# Advance Agility Workbook

*by Clean Run Productions*

## An Eight-Week Training Program for Dogs That Have Completed an Intermediate Agility Program

**Clean Run Productions**
35 Walnut Street, Turners Falls, MA 01376

## Advanced Agility Workbook

Published by    **Clean Run Productions**
        35 Walnut Street
        Turners Falls, MA 01376-2317
        413/863-8303

**Acquiring Editor and Chief Writer**   Bud Houston
**Editors**   Linda Mecklenburg and Monica Percival
**Contributors**   Nancy Gyes, Stuart Mah, Linda Mecklenburg, Monica Percival
**Book and Cover Design**   Monica Percival
**Cover Artwork**   Karen Gaydos, Jo Ann Mather, and Valerie Pietraszewska
**Book Illustrations**   Rebecca Cheek, Jaci Cotton, Karen Gaydos, Nancy Krouse-Culley, Bud Houston, Jo Ann Mather, Pascal Peng, and Valerie Pietraszewska
**Printing**   Hadley Printing Company

**ISBN** 0-9653994-2-7

# Contents

# *Program Director's Notes*

This workbook represents an eight-week instruction for dogs and handlers that have previously been introduced to obstacle sequencing and elementary handling techniques, either through the program described in the *Intermediate Agility Workbook* by Clean Run Productions or a comparable intermediate course. The exercises and discussions here are intended for the instructors of an advanced program. Pages are included that are suitable for handout material for the students in the program.

## Objectives of This Advanced Program

The objective of this program is to improve the working relationship between dog and handler, and to prepare the agility *team* for competition. This program places a fundamental emphasis on the handler keeping the dog's attention, and on improving the handler's skills in this sport.

While not explicitly stated in this advanced program, it is expected that the instructors of the advanced program will continue to stress the following concepts, which were important parts of both the introductory and intermediate agility programs:

- The handler will reward his dog for the performance of a contact obstacle in the descending contact zone and nowhere else. The dog is not allowed to leave the contact zone of the obstacle without the permission, a quiet release command, of the handler.

- The handler will be challenged to work the dog on the off-side as well as the heel-side.

- The dog will be encouraged to go away from the handler to work.

**NOTE:** Basic training methodologies for obstacle performance are *not* discussed in this workbook as they are covered in detail in the *Introductory Agility Workbook* published by Clean Run Productions. In addition, suggestions for solving specific obstacle performance problems are *not* discussed in this workbook as they are covered in detail in the *Intermediate Agility Workbook* published by Clean Run Productions.

## About the Logistics of an Advanced Program

While the presentation in this workbook may appear to suggest or endorse the one right way to conduct an advanced program, training programs for dog agility take a variety of forms. Programs differ in terms of basic training techniques, administration, length of program, and guidelines for admittance and graduation.

### Guidelines for Admittance

Dogs are eligible for this advanced program when:

- **The dog has successfully completed an approved intermediate agility program.** If a dog and handler did not complete *your* intermediate agility program, make sure that you find out details about their prior agility training and assess whether or not they have an appropriate background for making the transition to your advanced program. If you have any reservations about a student, you may want to consider requiring the student to take a private lesson with you. This will allow you to better acquaint yourself with both handler and dog, and give the handler a chance to familiarize himself with your training techniques.

- **You have received a complete application and pre-payment of the training fee.** Prior to the first class, the dog's owner should have submitted an application for enrollment, which should include the owner's signature, a release of liability, and proof of current vaccinations. Be sure you have a clearly stated policy regarding refunds (if any) for cancellation.

- **The dog demonstrates good control off-lead.** As in the introductory and intermediate agility programs, control should be determined as a pre-assessment. Students in an advanced agility program *must* have good off-lead control of their dogs or you will not be able to focus on teaching them more advanced concepts and handling skills. Students who need to focus on control do *not* belong in advanced agility program as they will disrupt the class. You should refer them for private help or keep them in your intermediate agility class.

## Guidelines for Graduation

At most training facilities, the advanced class is the end of the line, so to speak. There is no reason to graduate dogs because there is no other agility class for the dogs to attend. Advanced class is where the dogs will spend the rest of their agility careers, improving and maintaining their skills for competition. This is one of the reasons that it's so difficult to design an advanced program; students range from the handler/dog team fresh out of the intermediate program to the seasoned handler/dog team who just won a major competition or finished a title.

## What Your Students Should Bring to Class

When you confirm a dog's enrollment in your training program, use the opportunity to remind your students what they need to bring to class. Here's a good list for you to work with:

- A buckle collar or a quick release collar.

- A 4" or 6" tab lead.

- A 6' obedience lead.

- Lots of the dog's favorite food treats. Some people don't really know what their dog's favorite treat is. If you assess that a dog isn't particularly interested in the food motivator selected by his handler, suggest that the handler bring a *special* treat such as string cheese, Rollover™, Oinkeroll™, microwaved hotdogs, liver, etc.

- A toy motivator (such as a ball, a Frisbee™, or a squeaky toy).

- Water and a bowl for the dog.

- A hungry dog! For an evening agility class, recommend that your students delay the dog's dinner until after class. For classes earlier in the day, they should skip the dog's morning feeding. This tactic will make the dog's attention that much keener!

## How to Divide Your Classes

Each class session in this workbook has three working "sets". A set is the collection of equipment for which one instructor is responsible during the class. It is usually better, though certainly not required, for one instructor to remain with the same set of equipment throughout the class. The students, divided into groups, rotate from set to set during the class. Divide your class evenly—one group of students for each set.

The sets are intended to be worked simultaneously by a large class or consecutively by a small class. If you are working sets simultaneously, it's necessary to divide your students into logical groups. The best way to divide a class is by jump height. This allows dogs of the same jump height to work together so not a lot of time is spent adjusting bars.

**NOTE:**  Throughout this workbook we make reference to "big dogs" and "little dogs". In general, any dog that measures 16" or less at the shoulders is considered a little dog. Any dog measuring more than 16" is a big dog.

Another way to divide a class is by skill level. For example, if you use the data on the Progress Worksheets in this book to group together the dogs having difficulty with certain skills, it will be possible to fashion a more remedial program for just those dogs. Dogs that are advancing more quickly can be given a more advanced program.

If you divide into groups, the time students spend on each set should be carefully monitored; otherwise, it's possible that there won't be enough time to get to all the required sets. To make this work, one of your instructors must be assigned the task of keeping time. If there are three sets and three groups of students, for example, an hour should be divided into 20-minute working periods. The timekeeper will give a two-minute warning *prior* to each switch between sets and will announce clearly at the end of the 20 minutes that it is time to switch.

## Setting Up for Class

From day one, be an advocate for teaching your students the proper work ethic for participation in this sport. Setting up equipment is a lot of work. Get your students involved. If you get them used to the idea that you're going to do everything for them, they will soon come to expect you to continue to do so. Get them used to doing a share of the work and they will always expect to do their fair share.

One possibility is to require half of the class to come 30 minutes early to help move and set up equipment. Require the other half of the class to stay late to put equipment away and clean up the training site. Be prepared to get tough with students who won't do their fair share of work. Make them sit out a week if they don't help with the work!

## Cleaning Up After the Dogs

Encourage your students to exercise their dogs before coming to class. However, accidents are sometimes unavoidable. Your policy should be that the handler is responsible for immediately cleaning up after his dog.

Some programs require that students always be prepared for such an accident by carrying at least one plastic baggie in a pocket at all times. This ensures that the mess is quickly cleaned up and that it's not "lost" or stepped in while the handler is searching the training site for cleaning implements.

## Not Allowed!

By policy, you should not allow:

- **Aggressive dogs.** Dogs should not exhibit aggressiveness either towards other dogs or towards people.

- **Harsh training methods.**

- **Choke chains and pinch collars.**

- **Bitches in season.** Some clubs do not allow bitches in heat. Other clubs can function adequately if the bitch is diapered. You'll have to make the call.

- **Barking dogs.** Of course, all dogs bark. What you are guarding against here is the dog that barks without pause or purpose. This restriction is intended to placate neighbors that would be disturbed by a constantly barking animal as well as to make sure that instructors aren't struggling to be heard over the noise.

- **Dogs that run away.** If you can't catch 'em, you can't train 'em.

## Don't Forget Your Instructors

Being an instructor is sometimes a thankless job. Often instructors train other people's dogs at the expense of training their own. We advocate a policy that sets aside time and facilities for instructors to put their own dogs on the equipment. In an ideal world, your instructors should receive financial compensation for sharing their expertise and expending time and effort in support of your training program. An unpaid instructor can soon become an unhappy instructor.

*Artist: Jaci Cotton*

## How to Use This Workbook

This workbook includes pages that are designed for you to copy and distribute to your instructors and your students. For each week of the program, you will find student and instructor handouts, Progress Worksheets, and Facility Layouts that you can copy. The following sections explain how to best use each of these tools.

### Handouts

This workbook is designed so that pages can be copied as handouts. Handouts come in two forms:

- **Student Handouts**—Each week have ready for your students the pages labeled "Student Notes". Remember that your students will be avidly interested in anything they can get their hands on to read about this sport.

- **Instructor Handouts**—For each week of class, each instructor should receive the "Instructor Notes" with the Progress Worksheet for that week copied on the second side. Each instructor should also receive a copy of the exercise(s) for which he'll be responsible. Ideally, the instructors should receive their copies *at least* a week ahead of the scheduled class so they can mentally prepare for what they must do with their students.

    Instructors should get a copy of the Facility Layout for that week so they can direct the work in setting up the equipment for that lesson.

    Encourage your instructors to make notes about what works *and* what doesn't work in the training program. Your program will improve by the empirical knowledge they earn while conducting classes. An instructor will develop a keener eye for training and performance issues by keeping copious notes on the process.

### Progress Worksheets

On the back of each week's Instructor Notes is a worksheet—or if you prefer, a model for a worksheet—that is used to take attendance and track a dog's progress. Each week write the names of your students in the left column, along with their dogs' names. This will help you and the other instructors learn all the new names you need to learn. Also, each week, make appropriate progress notes in the space provided. This will help you and your instructors remember who needs help and in what areas, and assist in setting the difficulty of the exercises for next week's class.

### Facility Layouts and Facility Layout Worksheets

The Facility Layout is a design for placement of the obstacles on your training field. Some thought has been given to the ideal placement of the obstacles in the field, considering how dogs will move through each exercise and how dogs and their handlers might line up or queue at the start of each set.

In an ideal world, we all have two acres in which to set up our training sets. In the real world, however, many clubs do their training in limited spaces. It's conceivable that there won't be enough space to set up all exercises for a given week at the same time. If your agility area is smaller than the ideal field, you must design the facility layout for each week *prior* to class. For this reason, blank Facility Layout Worksheets have been provided. Feel free to make additional copies for your use.

Designing the facility layout is no small task, you will find. You have to be very thoughtful about how the obstacles are going to be set up. There should be enough room between sets so that dogs are not running into each other. This will be especially important when dogs are working off-lead. Consider too that only one dog will be working on a set at a time. You must leave room for dogs and their handlers to wait in line, and you must leave room for some kind of path for a dog finishing an exercise to get back to the end of the line.

## Acknowledgments

We thank all of the people who have made contributions to this *Advanced Agility Workbook*. A special thanks to Linda Mecklenburg and Monica Percival whose considerable skill and insight as agility instructors and seminar leaders are reflected in the philosophy of this book. Thanks also to Nancy Gyes and Stuart Mah for their contributions to the exercises in this program. We also want to say thanks to a wonderful corps of artists who have allowed us to use their work to brighten up these pages: Rebecca Cheek, Jaci Cotton, Karen Gaydos, Jo Ann Mather, Nancy Krouse-Culley, and Valerie Pietraszewska.

# *Curriculum*

Most of your students will be fresh out of the intermediate training program. In *that* program, students were introduced to obstacle sequencing and some basic handling techniques. In the advanced training program, you will continue to work on these skills and you will seek constant improvement in the dog and handler team.

This curriculum is intended to be representative of the type of work that should be *ongoing* at the advanced level. It is *not* intended to be a definitive text on advanced agility training. Creating such a text would be nearly impossible by virtue of the sheer volume that such a reference would occupy. Teaching advanced agility classes is *not* just a matter of learning a specific series of movements, any more than becoming a musician is just a matter of learning the scales. Today's advanced agility instructor must be a psychologist, an inductive scientist, a public speaker, a holistic health specialist, a personal trainer, and a philosopher. To speak to all of that would be a prodigious task indeed.

Advanced agility training must be dynamic, interactive, ever changing, and adaptable. You set up the obstacles, explain the purpose of the exercise, give away a tip or two, and then you step back and let your students have at it. The set represents a question you are asking your students—How will you handle this challenge? You and your instructors must observe the answers that your students give, and make appropriate comments and recommendations. Often, you will find that you need to redesign an exercise because it either does not create the intended challenge or meet the needs of your students. The instructors of an advanced agility program must be able to make changes "on the fly", simplifying exercises for dogs that are struggling and adding complexity to exercises for dogs *and* handlers that are ready for new challenges.

While this workbook provides you with a starting point for an advanced agility program, it is critical that you and your instructors keep expanding your knowledge of the sport and getting new training ideas—go to seminars, take private lessons from more experienced instructors, and read everything that you can get your hands on.

## Raising Obstacles During the Curriculum

During the intermediate program, you gradually raised the height of jumps and the other obstacles. However, dogs coming out of the intermediate program are still not working at their competition jump height. Therefore, this advanced program includes an eight-week program for raising jumps to competition height. The progress of dogs in the jump height program should be carefully monitored. Whichever instructor is responsible each week for the "Raising Jump Heights" exercise should make complete notes about how students are progressing.

## Working Sets

This program provides a half dozen weekly exercises that can be situated in physically separate sets or stations, allowing you to divide your class into groups that will get a good workout on the equipment and minimize standing around time. These sets require more field space than the sets in the introductory and intermediate programs. Unfortunately, reality is that as exercises get more complex and you add more obstacles to increase the dog's ability to sequence, you need more physical space. If you do not have enough space to set up all three stations simultaneously, you are going to have to limit the size of your advanced classes.

The program thoughtfully divides the set of equipment listed below into these three sets or stations. Any movement of equipment between exercises occurs only within the individual station.

- Dogwalk
- A-frame
- See-saw
- 12 single bar jumps
- 2 double bar spread hurdles
- Triple spread hurdle

- Long jump or broad jump
- Tire
- 10–12 weave poles
- 2 tables
- 2 pipe tunnels
- Collapsed tunnel

The following table summarizes the three sets you will work during each week of the eight-week program as well as the equipment that is required for each set.

| Set 1 | Set 2 | Set 3 |
|---|---|---|
| **Week 1** **Bedeviled** *Obstacles:* four winged jumps, long jump  **Turn** *Obstacles:* five winged jumps  *Note:* Major equipment movement is required between exercises. | **Pinwheel Peril 1 & 2** *Obstacles:* four winged jumps, pipe tunnel, tire, dogwalk, weave poles | **Perilous Pitch** *Obstacles:* four winged jumps, collapsed tunnel  **Raising Jump Heights** *Obstacles:* five winged jumps  *Note:* Major equipment movement is required between exercises. |
| **Week 2** **Discrimination** *Obstacles:* A-frame, winged jump, pipe tunnel  **Double Dragon** *Obstacles:* A-frame, four winged jumps, pipe tunnel, tire (or another winged jump)  *Note:* Minor equipment movement is required between exercises. | **Option Set 1 & 2** *Obstacles:* six winged jumps, tire (or another winged jump)  **Raising Jump Heights** *Obstacles:* five winged jumps  *Note:* Major equipment movement is required between exercises. | **Trouble and Double Trouble** *Obstacles:* three winged jumps, dogwalk, pipe tunnel, collapsed tunnel, triple spread hurdle, table  **Opening Sequence** *Obstacles:* two winged jumps, collapsed tunnel  *Note:* Minor equipment movement is required between exercises. |
| **Week 3** **Working Away and Change-Up** *Obstacles:* Dogwalk, winged jump, pipe tunnel, collapsed tunnel, table  **Subtle Deception and The Dodge** *Obstacles:* Dogwalk, winged jump, double spread hurdle, pipe tunnel | **Option Exercises** *Obstacles:* A-frame, three winged jumps, weave poles, table  **Raising Jump Heights/End Game** *Obstacles:* five winged jumps  *Note:* Major equipment movement is required between exercises. | **Mystery Exercise** *Obstacles:* weave poles, long jump, tire, see-saw  **Recalls** *Obstacles:* two winged jumps  *Note:* Major equipment movement is required between exercises. |
| **Week 4** **Playground and Playground Option** *Obstacles:* A-frame, two pipe tunnels, four winged jumps, tire | **Ken's Innovation and On the Other Hand** *Obstacles:* see-saw, three winged jumps | **Raising Jump Heights/End Game** *Obstacles:* five winged jumps, table |
| **Week 5** **Weave 'n the Wheel Exercises** *Obstacles:* five winged jumps and two short sets of weave poles  *Note:* Minor equipment movement is required between exercises. | **Run Around Sue and Run Around Sue Variation** *Obstacles:* one winged jump, tire, dogwalk, pipe tunnel, double spread hurdle  **Off-Side Sweep** *Obstacles:* A-frame, two nonwinged jumps  *Note:* Minor equipment movement is required between exercises. | **In Front** *Obstacles:* see-saw, table, four winged jumps  **Raising Jump Heights and End Game** *Obstacles:* five winged jumps, long jump, table  *Note:* Major equipment movement is required between exercises. |
| **Week 6** **Tunnel Turmoil 1 & 2** *Obstacles:* nonwinged jump, see-saw, two pipe tunnels, double spread hurdle, triple spread hurdle, weave poles | **180° Whoops** *Obstacles:* four winged jumps, tire  **Raising Jump Heights** *Obstacles:* four winged jumps, tire  *Note:* Major equipment movement is required between exercises. | **Walk Into Pinwheel Peril** *Obstacles:* three winged jumps, dogwalk, A-frame  **Blind Ascent** *Obstacles:* A-frame, two winged jumps  *Note:* Major equipment movement is required between exercises. |
| **Week 7** **Utility Agility** *Obstacles:* four winged jumps  **Raising Jump Heights** *Obstacles:* four winged jumps, tire, long jump, table  *Note:* Major equipment movement is required between exercises. | **Go Tunnel!** *Obstacles:* dogwalk, two winged jumps, double spread hurdle, collapsed tunnel, two pipe tunnels | **Murphy Shoulda Said It** *Obstacles:* three winged jumps, two nonwinged jumps, A-frame  **Depressed Bootlace** *Obstacles:* A-frame, five winged jumps  *Note:* Major equipment movement is required between exercises. |
| **Week 8** **Corner 1, 2 and 3** *Obstacles:* A-frame, weave poles, collapsed tunnel, three winged jumps  **Raising Jump Heights** *Obstacles:* five winged jumps  *Note:* Major equipment movement is required between exercises. | **Loop de Loops** *Obstacles:* dogwalk, four winged jumps, one nonwinged jump, table (or another nonwinged jump), pipe tunnel | **T Trouble and More T Trouble** *Obstacles:* see-saw, pipe tunnel, tire, table  **Oopsi! Change of Direction and Revisionist Oopsi!** *Obstacles:* six winged jumps  *Note:* Major equipment movement is required between exercises. |

# Week 1: Instructor Notes

If you ask a dozen instructors what troubles them most in delivering an on-going advanced training program for dog agility, ten of them will tell you that it is attempting to balance the disparate training objectives of individuals. Imagine yourself trying to design an advanced program for a class which includes each of the following:

- Velcro dogs—Dogs that won't work away from their handlers and are possibly reluctant even to leave the heel-side position.

- Speed demons—Very fast dogs that charge around the course recklessly, volunteering for any obstacle in their path.

- Unmotivated dogs—Dogs that aren't in any particular hurry no matter how much mom or dad cajoles or how great the reward.

*Artist: Jo Ann Mather*

These are only obvious examples of dogs with very different training needs. Having these dogs in the *same* class challenges you to develop a program that *advances* the training objectives of *each* dog.

If you are using the training sets from this workbook, then you are using "off-the-shelf" exercises. There's nothing wrong with this. However, each week you must take an additional step in which you consider the unique training requirements of the handlers and dogs who are in your class. Mentally review each exercise, keeping in mind the performance characteristics of your students. It is possible that you might *not* want to run all the dogs on a particular exercise, or that you might want to redesign elements of certain exercises for some dogs. For example, you might have the handlers of the speed demon dogs sit out when you're working on a "go-go-go" type of exercise that is intended to push dogs ahead, encourage speed, and build confidence. Alternatively, you might change the exercise for the speed demons and have them skip every other obstacle in the sequence so that those handler/dog teams focus on attention and control. Don't be afraid to innovate and make adjustments.

| | Set 1 | Set 2 | Set 3 |
|---|---|---|---|
| **Week 1** | **Bedeviled** <br> *Obstacles:* four winged jumps, long jump <br><br> **Turn** <br> *Obstacles:* five winged jumps <br><br> *Note:* Major equipment movement is required between exercises. | **Pinwheel Peril 1 & 2** <br> *Obstacles:* four winged jumps, pipe tunnel, tire, dogwalk, weave poles | **Perilous Pitch** <br> *Obstacles:* four winged jumps, collapsed tunnel <br><br> **Raising Jump Heights** <br> *Obstacles:* five winged jumps <br><br> *Note:* Major equipment movement is required between exercises. |

## Organizational Notes

Prior to class, get your instructors together for a briefing. Make sure that everyone has a copy of the exercises for the day. It's often a good idea to work one of your own dogs in each exercise with all of your instructors present so that everyone understands the curriculum.

Remind your instructors to make performance notes on the Progress Worksheets about the dogs and handlers working in the exercises they lead. These notes can be reviewed prior to next week's class so that all of the instructors know who is having difficulties with what obstacles or skills.

Start the new class with introductions all around. As your students introduce themselves, check them "present" on the Progress Worksheet (on the other side of this page). Don't forget to introduce yourself. After you welcome your students, take care of "housekeeping" items such as ground rules for moving equipment, cleaning up, etc.

Begin your training session by doing the control exercise on page 15 with all students. Then break into groups for the training sets if you're going to work multiple sets simultaneously.

# *Week 1: Progress Worksheet*

**Instructors:**                                         **Date:**

| Handler and Dog | Present | Notes |
|---|---|---|
| | | |
| | | |
| | | |
| | | |
| | | |
| | | |
| | | |
| | | |
| | | |
| | | |
| | | |
| | | |

GENERAL NOTES:

# Week 1: Facility Layout

One square = 10'

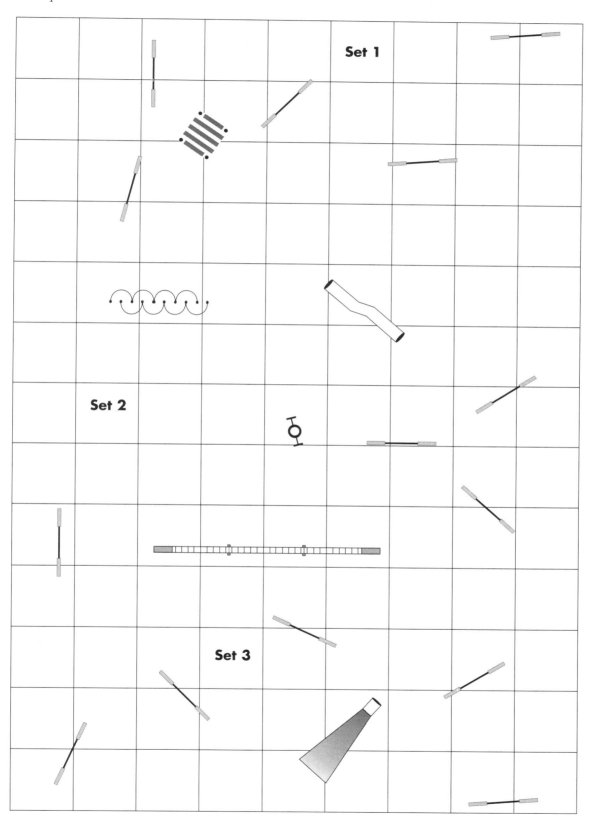

# Week 1: Facility Layout Worksheet

Design your Facility Layout using a 1" = 10' scale (standard agility template)

# Week 1: Exercises

Start the class by doing the control exercise with everyone. Then break into smaller groups if you're going to work the training sets simultaneously.

## Control Exercise

- With all of the dogs on-lead, have your students free heel the dogs in a "follow-the-leader" fashion through the field of equipment. Allow the dogs to sniff and inspect the equipment. Take your time. Let the dogs get any desire to sniff and explore out of their systems.

- Instruct your students that you will now do an attention exercise. The purpose of the exercise is to work on the *Come!* command with a bit of motivation added using the leash. Have everyone free heel their dogs on-lead simultaneously, but individually rather than in a follow-the-leader queue. About every ten seconds each handler should unexpectedly change direction, giving the dog a *Come!* command. If the dog doesn't immediately change direction to match the handler's new direction, the handler should give a crisp "pop" on the leash to remind the dog that the *Come!* is not optional. Tell your students that the ideal moment to change direction and command the dog to *Come!* is when the dog is approaching an obstacle or another dog.

End of exercise.

## Set 1

Your set consists of two exercises. Major equipment movement will be required between exercises. Brief your students immediately that they will be moving the equipment between exercises. You will lay the jump bars on the ground to indicate where to position jumps. Instruct your students to move the jump standards into place.

Balance your time with each group so that your students get approximately the same amount of work on each of the exercises.

### Bedeviled

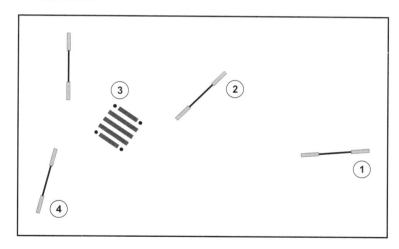

This exercise presents the long jump in a very ugly looking sequence. Regardless of whether you allow handlers to lead out or to begin on one side or the other, this is really going to test the dog and handler relationship.

What is the best approach to the long jump at #3? Immediately turning the dog left after jump #2? Or, by turning the dog right after jump #2 and then around a full 180° to face the long jump? There is no right answer. Try it both ways.

How does the handler's choice at the long jump impact the transition to jump #4? Can the handler directly attack jump #4 after the long jump or does he need to alter the dog's path for a better approach to the jump?

**NOTE:** A dog that enters the marking poles for the long jump through the front, but exits through one side or the other, has committed a refusal.

## Turn

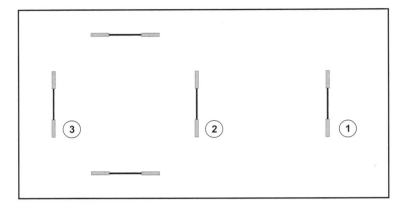

This is the quintessential change of direction exercise. It will help teach the handlers how pushing forward and hanging back can influence a dog's choice of direction, and it will help teach the dogs that they need to stay attentive to their handlers because going straight ahead isn't always the correct path!

While handlers may choose to work the dog on either side, do *not* allow handlers to lead out for this exercise.

- First, have the dogs do a simple, straight-ahead sequence over three jumps that are spaced approximately 20 feet apart. Notice that jumps #2 and #3 form two sides of a box. This configuration is sometimes called a "Hobday box" or "jumping square".

- Next, introduce a simple turn. After jump #2, the dog is required to turn right to jump #3.

- Finally, have the dog turn left after jump #2.

Many handlers will tell you that there is no way they will be able to get their dogs to turn in a sequence like this—especially since they just did another exercise which patterned their dogs to perform the three jumps in a row. Often they are right. A "green" dog has to learn to always check off with his handler for the correct sequence.

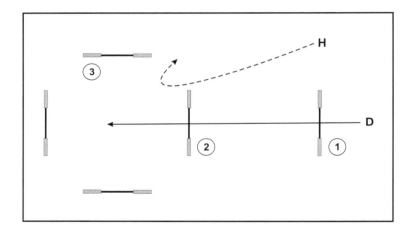

You can see in the illustration that the handler has pushed into the box of jumps with the dog. Usually, the dog's inability to turn is because the handler pushes too far forward—especially in the case of dogs that naturally have a lot of forward propulsion. The dog reacts to the handler's forward motion by pushing out to the jump in the direction of the handler's motion. Advise the handler to hang back from the box. There is no need to push all the way into the box. Indeed, pushing too far gives the dog the wrong signal.

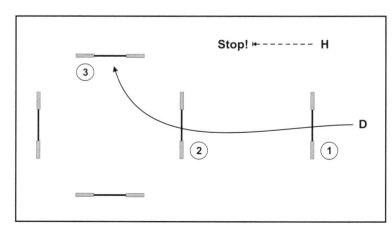

In this illustration, the handler is shown stopping—hanging back about halfway between jumps #1 and #2. Although you can have the handlers work this exercise with a healthy *Come!* command, you will probably discover that the dog will turn back in the direction of the handler, regardless of any command the handler gives. Consequently the handler's next task is to redirect the dog to jump #3.

# Set 2

Your set consists of two exercises that use the same equipment set-up. No equipment movement will be required; you'll just need to renumber the obstacles.

Balance your time with each group so that your students get approximately the same amount of work on each of the exercises.

You'll be working with the dogwalk, which should be at *full height*, in your set. Remind your students that they should reward their dogs (whether it's with food or with praise) *only* in the contact zone of the descent ramp. The dog is not permitted to leave the contact zone without a quiet release from his handler. If the dog bails off early, he should be picked up and placed back in the contact zone. At this stage, encourage your students to complete contact obstacles without giving a treat to the dog on the down-side contact every time. Instead, they will treat the dog in the down-side contacts on every other repetition or even every third repetition. However, whether or not food is being used for a particular repetition, your students should still ask the dog for an attentive wait in the contact zones and praise the dog for doing this correctly.

Your set also includes weave poles. Remind your students that they must work on weave poles at home. In class, you will continue to use regulation weave poles with channel wires as you did in the intermediate program. Beginning in Week 3, however, you will start to remove wires from the chute until only a single wire is left to help with entry. To prepare for competition, the dogs need to start seeing weave poles without wires in class.

## Pinwheel Peril 1 & 2

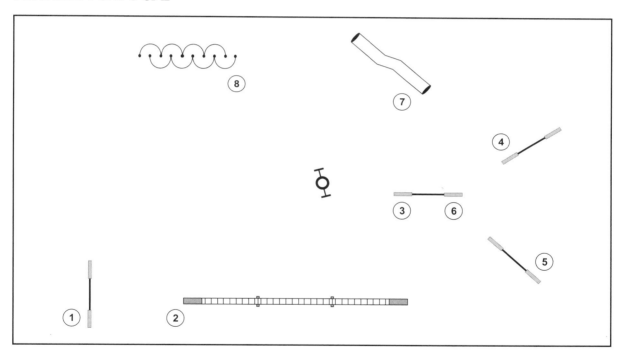

These exercises, which were designed by Stuart Mah of Stars and Stripes Agility in California, offer a number of challenges for your students. The #3–#5 configuration of jumps is referred to as a "pinwheel".

After leaving the dogwalk at #2, the handler must avoid a potential off-course over jump #5 on the way to jump #3. Some handlers will choose to get in front of the dog while its on the dogwalk (blocking jump #5) and then push the dog through the pinwheel of jumps with the dog on their left. How does this work?

How much trouble does the pipe tunnel give handlers during the transition from jump #3 to jump #4? What happens if the handler makes a tight left turn off the dogwalk and directly attacks jump #3?

Does the dogwalk pose an off-course possibility as the handlers make the transition from jump #5 to jump #6?

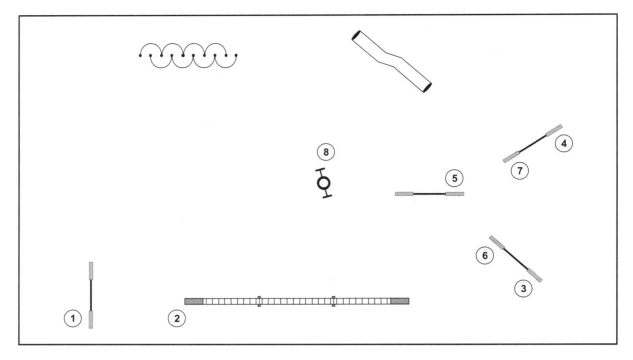

In this renumbered exercise, the handler has to get around the pinwheel twice and then avoid the pipe tunnel while going from jump #7 to the tire at #8.

Handlers who push through the pinwheel and try to stay to the right of jump #5 in making the transition from #7 to #8 may get into trouble. The results may be an off-course through the pipe tunnel, a hard call-off from the tunnel resulting in declining speed, or a ragged approach to the tire. Handlers who try to make it through this way might end up doing a lot of heeling.

The quickest and most efficient way to handle the transition from #7 to #8 may be to drop behind (toward the dogwalk) and to the left of jump #5 for the approach to the tire. This will put jump #5 between the handler and the dog, which will make many handlers nervous. However, encourage them to be confident and try this maneuver since. It should help pull the dog away from the tunnel and set up the dog for a straight approach to the tire.

## Set 3

Your set consists of two exercises. Major equipment movement will be required between exercises. Brief your students immediately that they will be moving the equipment between exercises. You will lay the jump bars on the ground to indicate where to position jumps. Instruct your students to move the jump standards into place.

You will be responsible for running the first part of the eight-week "Raising Jump Heights" program. Be sure to make careful notes of your students' progress so that whoever runs this exercise next week will be properly prepared and can make necessary adjustments.

Balance your time with each group so that your students get approximately the same amount of work on each of the exercises.

## Perilous Pitch

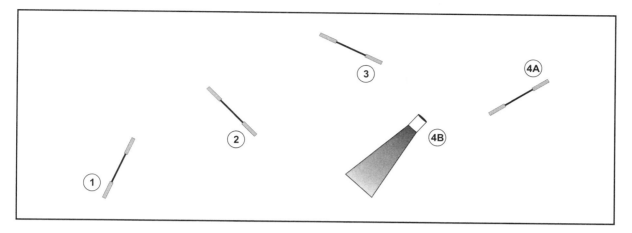

This exercise underscores the need to change a dog's direction *before* giving the command for the next obstacle. It will also help teach handlers how pushing forward and hanging back can influence a dog's choice of direction.

In each repetition, alternate which obstacle the dogs perform after jump #3—either the jump at #4A or the collapsed tunnel at #4B.

When going from jump #3 to the collapsed tunnel, just shouting *Tunnel!* will *not* help the handler turn the dog. In fact, many dogs will mistake the obstacle command as a confirmation that they should perform the obstacle directly in front of them, which will be the jump. The handler will need to use a strong *Come!* command and make sure that the dog is turned away from the off-course jump before giving a *Tunnel!* command. The handler will also have to be careful of the body language that he gives the dog—stepping too far into the sequence will surely pitch the dog out over the off-course jump.

## Raising Jump Heights

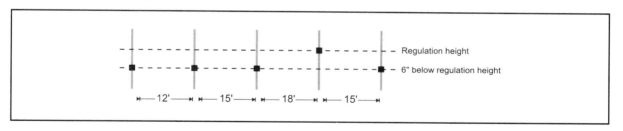

In the intermediate agility program, the goal was to gradually raise jump heights until the dogs were able to perform exercises with the jumps set at 6" below their competition height. One of the immediate objectives when a dog enters the advanced program is to train the dog to jump at his competition height—this height will be different for each dog, depending on the dog's height at the withers and the agility organization(s) under which the handler plans to show. For example, a dog that is over 21" at the withers must jump 30" in USDAA® competition. However, this same dog would jump only 24" under AKC® or NADAC rules.

To train a dog to jump *happily* and *confidently* at his competition height, you need to implement a planned program for raising jump heights. The eight-week "Raising Jump Heights" program described in this workbook is designed for dogs that are *at least* 18 months old. In addition, the dogs should be fit before embarking on this type of training program. Dogs that are overweight or out of condition should not participate.

This exercise introduces the dog to a regulation height jump by inserting this jump into a series of lower jumps. The other jumps in the series are set 6" below the dog's regulation jump height. The jumps are presented to the dog at varied intervals. This spacing is designed to allow the dog to build speed and stride on the approach to the regulation height jump (the fourth jump).

**NOTE:** For the other exercises this week, the dogs should continue jumping at 6" below their competition height.

Have each dog and handler do at least one repetition of each of the following:

- Run with the dog on the heel-side over the sequence of jumps.

- Run with the dog on the off-side over the sequence of jumps.

- Leave the dog in a sit-stay behind the first jump, lead out to the third jump, call the dog over the first three jumps, and then complete the sequence running with the dog on the heel-side (handler's left).

- Leave the dog in a sit-stay behind the first jump, lead out to the third jump, call the dog over the first three jumps, and then complete the sequence running with the dog on the off-side (handler's right).

- Leave the dog in a sit-stay behind the first jump, lead out past the last jump, and call the dog over all of the entire line of jumps.

**IF A DOG REFUSES THE REGULATION HEIGHT JUMP:** Put the dog on a program of incremental increases in jump height. Begin with the fourth jump in the series set at 6" under the dog's regulation height and the other jumps in the line set at 8"–12" under the dog's regulation height. Incrementally raise the jumps only 2" at a time. The handler should work with the dog for two days or more for each 2" increase. It's clear that this should be done as homework. You cannot raise a dog to regulation height using an incremental method in one class hour per week.

Keep an eye out for the possibility that the dog may be lame or overweight, or for some other reason does not like jumping regulation height. (See "Identifying Motivation Problems" on page 120 in the Appendix.)

If you believe that the dog is fit and healthy and remedies (see the *Intermediate Agility Workbook* for remedial work for jumping problems) aren't working with a particular dog, you might consider recommending that the handler postpone the program to raise the dog's jump height for another month or two. The dog's confidence could certainly be a factor. A dog moving too slowly to gather sufficient momentum to clear the jump, or stopping in front of the jump altogether, is a sign that the dog lacks confidence. The dog's attitude about jumping is important. You want the dog to be happy and confident. Many people are guilty of assuming that dogs are natural jumpers. Some dogs are, but many are not and require a great deal of time and training to work them up to jumping at their regulation height.

*The hydrant jump was a favorite with the dogs. Artist: Jaci Cotton*

# Week 1: Student Notes

At this point, your dog should understand the basic performance that you are asking for in the weave poles. Now it's time to begin a thoughtful program to build the confidence, speed, and reliability that you will need for competition. Once a week for part of an hour is *not* enough time on the weave poles to do this. You're probably tired of hearing this, but you *must* practice the weave poles at home if you are serious about competing in this sport!

Work several times a day with your dog on the weave poles for no more than five or ten minutes a session. It is your responsibility to ensure that your dog succeeds, your exercises end on a positive note, and your dog is confident and happy and supremely pleased with himself for figuring out what it was he had to do.

## Weave Pole Entry Exercises

*Artist: Karen Gaydos*

These first two exercises are simple approaches that allow you to lead out and call your dog into the weave poles. Each jump presents the dog with a strikingly different approach to the poles. However, notice that you maintain basically the same "post up" position for each approach—that position which is ideal for you to guide your dog into the weave poles.

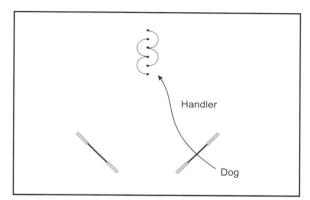
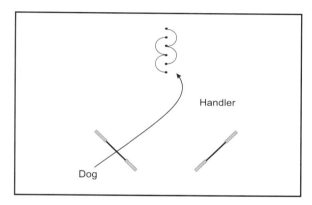

Next move with your dog, running alongside as the dog alternately begins the sequence with the left jump and then the right jump. Notice in the illustrations that the handling path seems significantly longer when approaching the weave poles from the left jump, as compared to the right jump. A left side approach to the weave poles means that *you* have the longer outside path, while the dog has the shorter inside path.

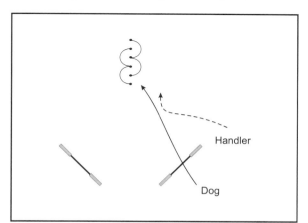
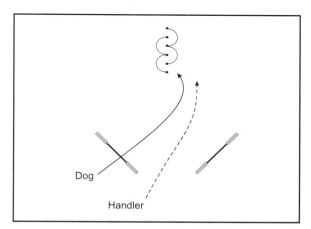

As you practice these exercises during the week, increase the challenge by drawing a box around the weave poles about 8' away. Work *outside* of this box as your dog performs the weave poles.

# Preparing for Distance Work

The exercises on this page begin a series that is intended to help you teach your dog some of the basic skills necessary for getting ready for advanced distance work. While you will practice these skills during your weekly agility classes, like the weave poles, they are something that you need to work on at home in order to see real progress. These exercises are also designed to improve the working relationship between dog and handler. They will help you work on the voice and body signals that you use to communicate your intentions to the dog; and they will help the dog to get familiar with these signals so that he knows what you want from him.

The commands *Come!* and *Get Out!* convey directional movement relative to *your* position to the dog. *Come!* is used to cause the dog to move laterally towards your position and *Get Out!* is used to cause the dog to move laterally away from your position. The following exercises will help you work on these important commands.

## Teaching *Come!* on the Run

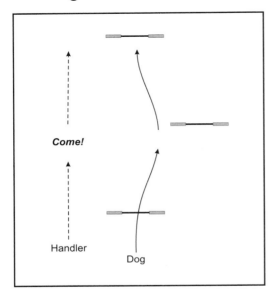

In this first exercise, you will run with your dog as the dog performs two jumps that are in a straight line. A "dummy" or a trap jump is set nearly (but not quite) in the dog's path. To avoid the dummy jump, use the *Come!* command to convey to your dog to come in towards you so that you can move past the jump.

While your dog might initially be tempted by the dummy jump, your *Come!* command conveys to the dog to come away from the jump. If your dog does take the dummy jump, withhold all praise or respond only with an unemotional *No!* or *Wrong!*. Then turn around and return to the starting position for the exercise. Repeat the exercise. Leave it to the dog to sort out what earns him praise and reward, and what does not.

Practice this at least once a day for two or three days. The dog should jump no more than 20 times per training session. Then work on the next exercise for the rest of the week.

## *Get Out!*

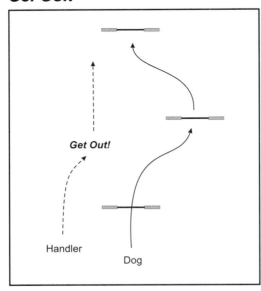

Having worked on *Come!*, it's time to work on the reciprocal command—*Get Out!* The illustration shows that you initially take a path parallel to the dog's path. Then you abruptly step in towards the dog (encroaching on the dog's space), give a hand signal towards the offset jump, and command the dog to *Get Out!*. This will push the dog away from you towards the jump. As the dog's nose turns towards the second jump, give a *Jump!* command. After the second jump, call the dog to *Come!* and then give a *Jump!* for the third jump.

If your dog refuses the offset jump, withhold all praise or respond only with an unemotional *No!* or *Wrong!*. Then turn around and return to the starting position for the exercise. Repeat the exercise. Leave it to the dog to sort out what earns him praise and reward, and what does not.

Practice this at least once a day (more if possible) for two or three days. The dog should jump no more than 20 times per training session.

# Week 2: Instructor Notes

If the handler expects to be an equal member of the agility team, he has a number of responsibilities. These can be summarized as keeping track of the course and communicating the course sequence to the dog. The skills necessary for doing this are far more complicated than they appear at first glance and give the handler a lot of things to think about as he directs his dog around an exercise or a course in competition.

You have the happy job not only to introduce the finer points of handling to your students, but to nag them over and over again about these details. Expect to repeat yourself dozens of times for each student. Just because a student hears you say something, does not mean that the jewel of wisdom was committed to long term memory, or even understood.

*Artist: Jo Ann Mather*

Often a dog and handler team's working relationship can be improved by looking at simple elements of the handler's attitude and posture. Here's a short list:

- **Hand signals**—A hand signal should be used to point to the correct obstacle in sequence. The signal should be a flag to the dog to take a particular path and *not* be a pantomime of feeding the dog a treat. The handler should use the hand closest to the dog and to the obstacle to be performed. The handler's hand must be within the dog's field of vision.

- **Voice**—The handler's voice should be loud enough for the dog to hear and emphatic enough to get the dog's attention, but not so loud or high-pitched that it stresses or overexcites the dog. The handler should minimize the number of words he uses. Typically, the dog's name is *not* required. A directional command, repeated as many times as necessary, followed by the command for the next obstacle should be sufficient. A command must be timed to give the dog enough time to react to it. Too often commands are given too late.

- **Handler's body**—The direction the handler's body is facing communicates a lot to the dog. Watch for handlers whose frames are turned perpendicular to the flow of the course. This confuses the dog. Also watch for handlers who crouch. The handler should have upright posture and should not bend over the dog.

- **Motion**—In most circumstances, a handler should keep moving. Many dogs will slow down when the handler slows down. So, if the handler is slowing down to wait for the dog, then the dog will slow down further, making the handler go even slower, which slows the dog down even more...you get the point.

| | Set 1 | Set 2 | Set 3 |
|---|---|---|---|
| **Week 2** | **Discrimination** *Obstacles:* A-frame, winged jump, pipe tunnel<br><br>**Double Dragon** *Obstacles:* A-frame, four winged jumps, pipe tunnel, tire (or another winged jump)<br><br>*Note:* Minor equipment movement is required between exercises. | **Option Set 1 & 2** *Obstacles:* six winged jumps, tire (or another winged jump)<br><br>**Raising Jump Heights** *Obstacles:* five winged jumps<br><br>*Note:* Major equipment movement is required between exercises. | **Trouble and Double Trouble** *Obstacles:* three winged jumps, dogwalk, pipe tunnel, collapsed tunnel, triple spread hurdle, table<br><br>**Opening Sequence** *Obstacles:* two winged jumps, collapsed tunnel<br><br>*Note:* Minor equipment movement is required between exercises. |

## Organizational Notes

Review the progress notes from week one. Ask your instructors if the exercises for week one were too hard or too easy for the class. If so, should today's exercises be modified in any way? Make note of any modifications to exercises in your master workbook. These notes will provide valuable intelligence for future classes.

Your instructors should read "Crosses, Changes and Switches" beginning on page 129 in the Appendix. Many of this week's working sets (and future week's) make use of these basic handling skills.

# *Week 2: Progress Worksheet*

**Instructors:**                                             **Date:**

| Handler and Dog | Present | Notes |
| --- | --- | --- |
|  |  |  |
|  |  |  |
|  |  |  |
|  |  |  |
|  |  |  |
|  |  |  |
|  |  |  |
|  |  |  |
|  |  |  |
|  |  |  |
|  |  |  |
|  |  |  |

GENERAL NOTES:

# Week 2: Facility Layout

One square = 10'

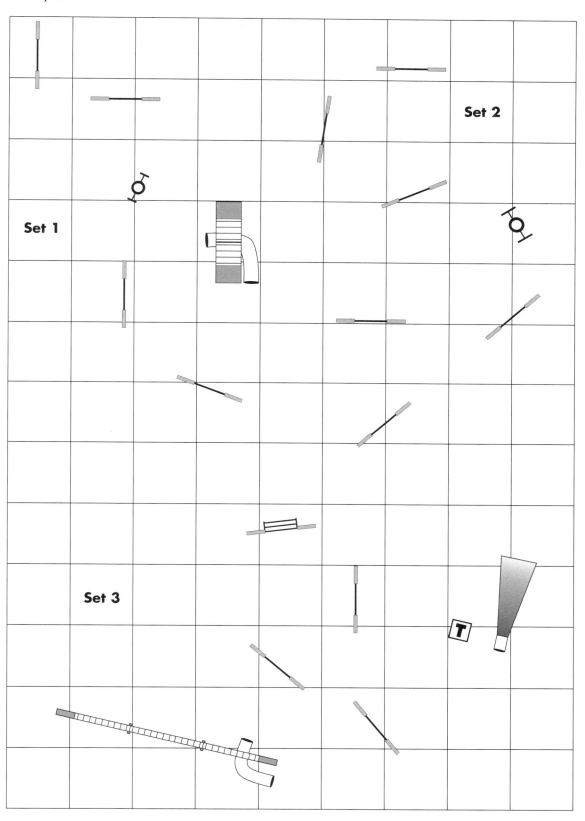

Set 1

Set 2

Set 3

T

# Week 2: Facility Layout Worksheet

Design your Facility Layout using a 1" = 10' scale (standard agility template)

# Week 2: Exercises

Start the class by doing the control exercise with everyone. Then break into smaller groups if you're going to work the training sets simultaneously.

## Control Exercise

- With all of the dogs on-lead, have your students free heel the dogs in a "follow-the-leader" fashion through the field of equipment. Allow the dogs to sniff and inspect the equipment. Take your time. Let the dogs get any desire to sniff and explore out of their systems.

- Instruct your students to heel the dogs at attention into a long line. You need 8' to 10' between dogs.

- Have your students leave the dogs in a down-stay and walk as far away from their dogs as they are comfortable. Whether that's across the field, or just to the end of the dog's lead, is entirely up to the owner.

- Recall the dogs *one* at a time. Each handler commands his dog to *Come!*. With any luck, the right dog will get up and come directly to the handler. If the dog does not do so, the handler will go and collect his dog. If the wrong dog comes, that dog's handler will collect his dog and put him back in a down with the other dogs.

- Praise and hold on to the dog until everyone has recalled their dogs.

End of exercise.

## Set 1

Your set consists of two exercises. Minor equipment movement (one jump) will be required between exercises.

You'll be working with the A-frame in your set. In the intermediate class, it was recommended that you gradually increase the height of the A-frame to 6' by the end of the program. In the advanced program, you will keep working with the A-frame at this height, unless you have students who intend to compete in USDAA® events. For these students, you will need to allow time to do some repetitions of each exercise with the A-frame set at 6' 3". Remind your students that they should reward their dogs (whether it's with food or with praise) *only* in the contact zone of the descent ramp. The dog is not permitted to leave the contact zone without a quiet release from his handler. If the dog bails off early, he should be picked up and placed back in the contact zone.

Balance your time with each group so that your students get approximately the same amount of work on each of the exercises.

### Discrimination

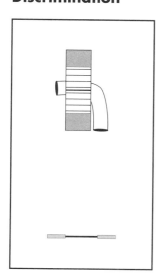

This exercise allows your students to work on possible handling solutions to this typical on-course dilemma:

1. **Blocking**—The handler stands in front of the undesirable obstacle and uses his body and arms to signal to the correct obstacle.

2. **Body magnet**—The handler positions himself on the same side as the obstacle to be performed, believing that his dog will do the obstacle closest to its handler.

3. **Directionals**—The handler uses directional commands to *drive* his dog to the correct obstacle, for example, *Jump! Go Right! Tunnel!*.

4. **True discrimination**—The handler has taught his dog the names of all the obstacles and knows that his dog will perform the one he commands.

Introduce each of these handling possibilities to your students, and then allow them to pick their own poison.

Have your students do one repetition of each of the following approaches to this exercise:

- Lead out and use blocking to put the dog on the A-frame.

- Lead out and use body magnet to put the dog on the A-frame.

- Run with the dog (no lead-out) and use blocking to put the dog on the A-frame.

- Run with the dog (no lead-out) and use body magnet to put the dog on the A-frame.

- Lead out and use blocking to put the dog in the pipe tunnel.

- Lead out and use body magnet to put the dog in the pipe tunnel.

- Run with the dog (no lead-out) and use blocking to put the dog in the pipe tunnel.

- Run with the dog (no lead-out) and use body magnet to put the dog in the pipe tunnel.

## Double Dragon

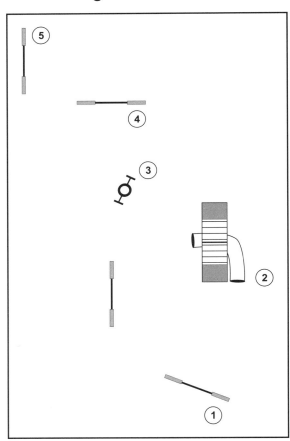

This exercise combines the discrimination challenge you worked on previously with a continued handling problem.

The set allows for very poetic and graceful changes of direction between dog and handler. The handler crosses behind the dog at the tire, pulling the dog right to jump #4; and then crosses behind the dog again, pulling the dog left over jump #5.

Note that the angle of approach to the discrimination problem is not "flat" as it was in the previous exercise. This set-up makes using body magnet problematical. Is it possible for the handler to work on the right side of the tunnel and then successfully run around behind the A-frame in time to call his dog through the tire? Well, you can bet *someone* is going to try it.

If the handler pushes or blocks the dog into the pipe tunnel, can he beat the dog to the other end of the tunnel and cross in front of the dog before it exits from the tunnel? This puts the dog on the handler's left for #3 and #4. Have your students try it this way and see what happens.

Make up your own sequences for this set of obstacles.

# Set 2

Your set consists of three exercises. The first two exercises use the same equipment with movement of only the tire. However, major equipment movement will be required between the second and third exercises. Brief your students immediately that they will be moving the equipment between exercises. You will lay the jump bars on the ground to indicate where to position jumps. Instruct your students to move the jump standards into place.

You will be responsible for running the second part of the eight-week "Raising Jump Heights" program. Be sure to make careful notes of your students' progress so that whoever runs this exercise next week will be properly prepared and can make necessary adjustments.

Balance your time with each group so that your students get approximately the same amount of work on each of the exercises.

## Option Set 1 & 2

This is a great set for fine tuning communications between handler and dog.

In the exercise illustrated on the left, there are two possible #3 obstacles. In each repetition, alternate which obstacle the dog performs after jump #2—either the jump at #3A or the tire at #3B.

Also alternate the position that the handler starts in. Have each handler perform both variations of the exercise starting with the dog on the right, the dog on the left, and with a lead-out.

In the exercise illustrated on the right, note that the tire has been moved. This time there are three possible #4 obstacles. Again, alternate *not only* the closing obstacle for each repetition, but the position from which the handler starts the exercise. Have the handler try it with the dog on right, the dog on the left, a lead-out beyond jump #1, a lead-out beyond jump #2, and a lead-out beyond jump #3.

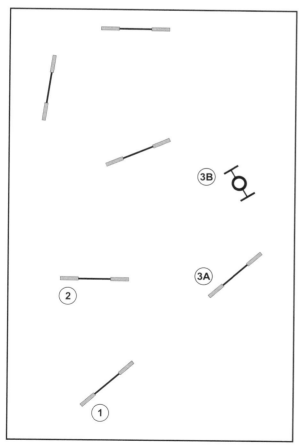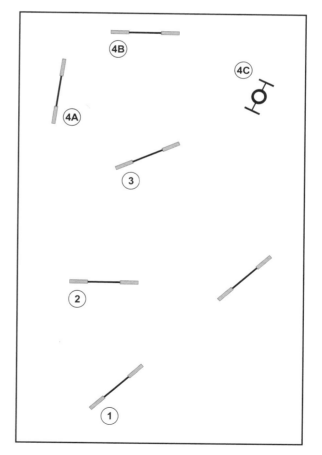

## Raising Jump Heights

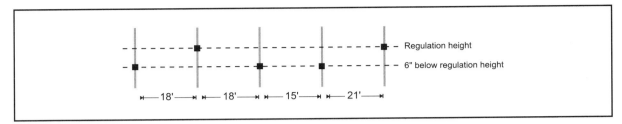

This exercise includes two regulation height jumps in a series of lower jumps. The other jumps in the series are set 6" below the dog's regulation jump height. The jumps are presented to the dog at varied intervals. This spacing is designed to allow the dog to build speed and stride on the approach to the regulation height jumps (the second and fifth jumps).

**NOTE:** For the other exercises this week, the dogs should continue jumping at 6" below their competition height.

Have each dog and handler do at least one repetition of each of the following:

• Run with the dog on the heel-side over the sequence of jumps.

• Run with the dog on the off-side over the sequence of jumps.

• Leave the dog in a sit-stay behind the first jump, lead out to the third jump, call the dog over the first three jumps, and then complete the sequence running with the dog on the heel-side.

• Leave the dog in a sit-stay behind the first jump, lead out to the third jump, call the dog over the first three jumps, and then complete the sequence running with the dog on the off-side.

• Leave the dog in a sit-stay behind the first jump, lead out past the last jump, and call the dog over all of the entire line of jumps.

**IF A DOG REFUSES THE REGULATION HEIGHT JUMPS:** Back up to the first week of the program, using only one regulation height jump in the sequence.

Keep an eye out for the possibility that the dog may be lame or overweight, or for some other reason does not like jumping regulation height.

If you believe that the dog is fit and healthy and remedies (see the *Intermediate Agility Workbook* for remedial work for jumping problems) aren't working with a particular dog, you might consider recommending that the handler postpone the program to raise the dog's jump height for another month or two. The dog's confidence could certainly be a factor. A dog moving too slowly to gather sufficient momentum to clear the jump, or stopping in front of the jump altogether, is a sign that the dog lacks confidence.

# Set 3

Your set consists of three exercises. The first two exercises use the same equipment. However, minor equipment movement will be required between the second and third exercises.

Your set includes the dogwalk. Remind your students that they should reward their dogs (whether it's with food or with praise) *only* in the contact zone of the descent ramp. The dog is not permitted to leave the contact zone without a quiet release from his handler. If the dog bails off early, he should be picked up and placed back in the contact zone.

Balance your time with each group so that your students get approximately the same amount of work on each of the exercises.

## Trouble

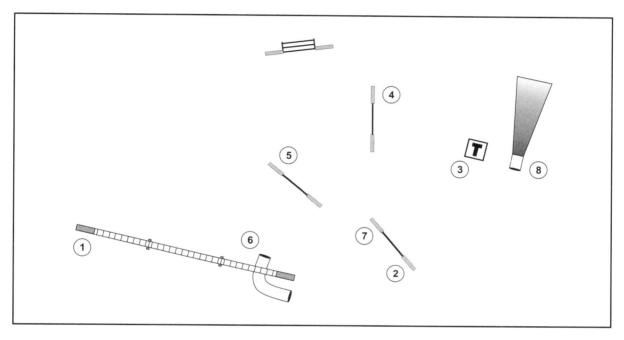

In this exercise, the magic *Come!* command should be adequate to bend the dog away from the tunnel, to the table, in the transition from #2 to #3. If the handler is "oversupervising" the dog, he could push the dog out to the collapsed tunnel. The handler will want to hang back enough to compel the dog to turn to the table.

The sequence of #6 through #8 is a bit trickier. Have the handler try blocking the table and pushing the dog out to the collapsed tunnel by encroaching on the dog's path and using a *Get Out!* command; this is just the opposite of the strategy to get the dog to turn to the table.

Is there another way to get the dog into the collapsed tunnel? After putting the dog into the pipe tunnel at #6, have the handler cross to the right side of jump #7 so that the dog will be in heel position coming out of the tunnel. This allows the handler to use body magnet attraction to pull the dog away from the off-course table and get the dog into the collapsed tunnel at #8.

If you have time, alter the sequence, making the table #8 and the collapsed tunnel #3. How does this affect the handling challenge in the set?

## Double Trouble

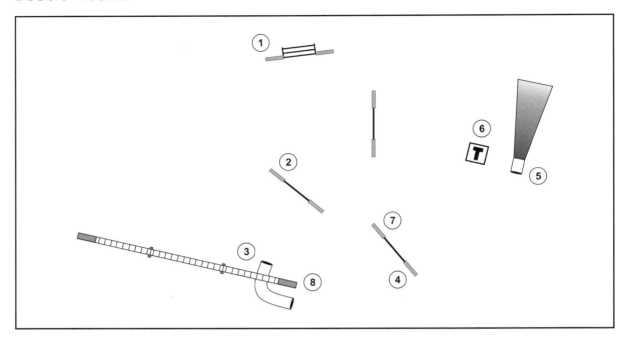

This exercise features *two* discrimination problems: one at quick time (dogwalk/pipe tunnel) and the other with table punctuation (table/collapsed tunnel).

Do not allow your students to lead out in this exercise.

A really fast dog will beat his handler to the table/tunnel challenge. How does this handler push his dog out to the collapsed tunnel?

What does the handler have to do to avoid the pipe tunnel and get his dog on the dogwalk at #8?

If the handler can leave his dog on the table and take a lead-out during the table count, he can get in a much better position to direct the dog to the dogwalk. If the handler has to stay with his dog to ensure that the dog remains in a down position (or a sit), he will most likely be forced to take an inside—body magnet—position to influence the dog to turn right, towards the handler, and onto the dogwalk.

# Opening Sequence

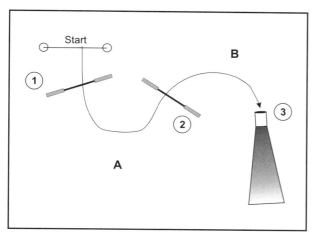

*Figure 1*

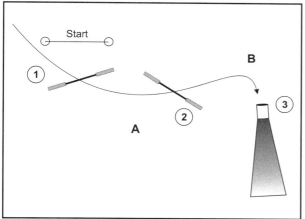

*Figure 2*

Your students will approach this sequence with varying success and fluidity.

There are three handling factors that influence how the sequence will be performed:

- **Lead-out advantage**—Handlers who lead-out and position themselves directly in the dog's path, as shown by handling position "A" in Figure 2, will be able to turn the dog very efficiently after jump #1 and then send the dog over jump #2.

  Alternatively, if the handler *sends* the dog over the first jump, he can take a lead-out advantage past jump #2 by shifting sideways towards the tunnel to handler position "B" in either figure. This will pull the dog towards the handler over jump #2.

- **Setting up the dog**—Figure 1 shows the handler rather thoughtlessly setting up the dog at the start line square to jump #1, ensuring a loopy and time-consuming sequence.

  Figure 2 shows the handler setting up the dog at the start line for a more thoughtful and efficient path over the first two jumps.

- **Voice commands**—Many handlers do not time their change of direction commands well. This could result in the dog running 10 or 12 yards longer than necessary in this sequence. From handler position "A" in either figure, the handler needs a well-timed *Come!* as the dog is in the air over jump #2. Waiting until the dog has landed and run five yards is too late.

  The handler who sends the dog over the first jump has to time the *Come!* command as the dog is in the air over the jump. The handler must then move laterally to handler position "B" to pull the dog over jump #2, and then he must push the dog into the tunnel. Again, waiting until the dog has landed to give a command will cause the dog to cover more ground than necessary.

# Week 2: Student Notes

Many of us who have done obedience training come to believe that our dogs should *always* work on our left—the heel-side. Did you know that in obedience, the original purpose of working dogs on the left is so that we can hold the dog's leash in our left hand to free our right hand for doing things like opening doors and shaking hands—*because so many of us are right handed!* Of course, in the tyranny of a right-handed world, we even expect this performance of left-handed individuals in obedience.

The idea of trying to work dogs exclusively on the heel-side in agility is pretty silly because we don't do agility with our dogs on leash (unless we are practicing some kind of very fundamental performance). So, we don't need to give that particular excuse power over us.

During obedience training, *the dog* will also come to believe that the left side is the "proper" side and will become confused when the handler gets on the "wrong" side. You can overcome this confusion only by doing a significant number of repetitions of the weave poles (or any other agility obstacle, for that matter) while working the dog on your right.

*Artist: Karen Gaydos*

## Off-Side Weave Work

This exercise is shamelessly crafted to squeeze two repetitions of the weave poles out of one simple sequence. The tunnel is a fast obstacle so you're not going to have much time to think about position or movement or getting a command out for the dog. Think about how you want to handle the sequence *before* you attempt to run the dog.

If you haven't acquired a tunnel yet, it's time to do so! You can order an inexpensive child's play tunnel that will suit your agility needs just fine, from most children's and educational mail order catalogs or you buy one at most large toy stores.

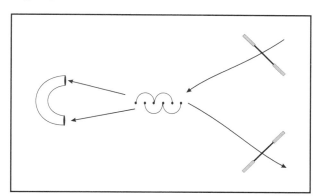

Perform the first three obstacles with the dog on your left side and then change sides while the dog is in the tunnel. This means that you'll do heel-side weave poles on the first pass and off-side weave poles on the way back.

Next, reverse sides so that you perform the first pass through the weave poles with the dog on your right side and then return through the weave poles with the dog on your left side.

Practice this exercise both ways for a few minutes each day this week.

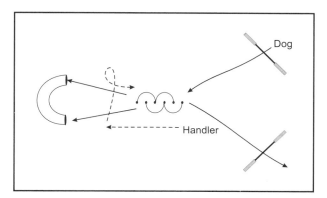

If you are ready for another handling challenge, try working the dog on your right side *both* going up through sequence and coming back. You can either start with the dog on your right behind the first jump, or you can lead out to the position shown in the illustration and call the dog over the first jump. As soon as you commit the dog into the tunnel, run to the other side of the tunnel and turn to your left (towards the dog). When the dog exits the tunnel, he will be on your right side. This fancy maneuver is often referred to as a "counter-rotation".

# Preparing for Distance Work

Unlike the directional commands *Come!* and *Get Out!*, some directional commands are *not* relative to the handler's position, but rather absolute in terms of the dog's position and movement. The *Go!* command, for instance, means that the dog should continue on his present path.

The easiest way to begin training this command is to set up a jump and a table. You can leave a food goodie on the table for the dog and make him appreciate going away from you to perform that obstacle.

If you don't have a regulation table then get creative and find something that can safely serve as a pause table.

## Absolute *Go!*

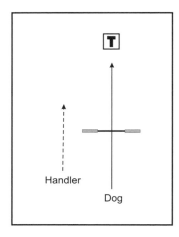

In this exercise you use a jump and a table. Put bait on the table for *each* repetition. You want the dog equating the table with happy things, like eating his favorite goodie.

Begin by putting your dog over the jump and then running with your dog to the table. As the dog "gets it" and understands that he's going to be rewarded each time he gets up on the table, you can begin to hang back and let him go ahead of you. After each repetition, hang back another step until you are sending the dog over the jump and onto the table without even taking a single step forward.

You can add excitement and expectation to the exercise by actually restraining your dog. Hold him at his hips and tell him *Ready? Ready? Ready! Go!* and then release him. He'll love the game and will bound away towards the table at top speed when you let him go.

It would be useful to have someone to help you with this exercise in case the dog decides that it's more economical to run around the jump between him and the table and the food. Your assistant can quickly remove the food from the table, depriving the dog of the treat for the improper performance.

Remember you don't ever want to give your dog an emotional correction for failing to do the exercise correctly. This could turn him off to the work and make him want to go in the house and sulk.

Do this exercise at least once a day for two or three days.

If the dog is doing well, add a second jump. When you add a jump, however, be sure to begin by running with the dog as he performs the obstacles. Then you can start gradually hanging back with each repetition.

If you continue to practice this exercise over the next few weeks, you can continue adding jumps until you are able to send the dog to the table over five jumps. Remember, each time you add a jump, start over from step one.

# Week 3: Instructor Notes

What do you do with a distracted dog? This is a dog who basically ignores the handler and goes on his merry way sniffing this and that, investigating birds, marking territory, visiting, and just about anything but heeding the handler's imploring attempts at communication.

This is a dog and handler team that needs to work on some "who's the boss" exercises. The goal of this work is *not* to compel the dog to "obey orders" through chastisement or harsh corrections, but rather to convince the dog that it's worthwhile and pleasant to pay attention to his handler so that the dog willingly and happily ignores distractions. Advise any of your students with this problem that they have to do some homework. This isn't likely to be cured on the agility field.

*Artist: Karen Gaydos*

Tell the handler to take the dog for a walk. Any time the dog sniffs or hauls on the lead, the handler should *silently* turn without warning and hurry in the opposite direction. Of course the dog is jerked away from the distraction and forced for that moment to pay the handler some attention. When the dog turns and moves towards the handler, he will praise the dog delightfully, celebrate, and reward the dog.

Like so many things, consistency and commitment are the keys. The handler has to get up off the couch and go on frequent walks with the dog. The about-face correction to the distracted dog has to be quiet and unexpected. The reward has to be profuse and happy. The student must be so committed to this kind of program that the problem can be solved in several weeks. It can't be a long, drawn out program with 15 minutes worth of commitment every two weeks. That's no commitment at all.

Once your student has worked on the homework and the dog understands the drill, you can have the handler apply the same program in class. Whenever the dog starts acting distracted in practice, instruct the handler to put the dog back on-lead and work on unexpected turns until the dog is focusing on the handler.

|  | Set 1 | Set 2 | Set 3 |
|---|---|---|---|
| **Week 3** | **Working Away and Change-Up** *Obstacles:* Dogwalk, winged jump, pipe tunnel, collapsed tunnel, table | **Option Exercises** *Obstacles:* A-frame, three winged jumps, weave poles, table | **Mystery Exercise** *Obstacles:* weave poles, long jump, tire, see-saw |
|  | **Subtle Deception and The Dodge** *Obstacles:* Dogwalk, winged jump, double spread hurdle, pipe tunnel | **Raising Jump Heights and End Game** *Obstacles:* five winged jumps *Note:* Major equipment movement is required between exercises. | **Recalls** *Obstacles:* two winged jumps *Note:* Major equipment movement is required between exercises. |

## Organizational Notes

Review the notes from the Week 2 Progress Worksheets with all of your instructors. Devise a plan for doing remedial work with dogs or handlers whose problems may cause delays in today's training plan. Sometimes it is necessary to group problem students together so that exercises can be simplified and remedial training steps can be taken without disturbing the work of more advanced dogs and handlers.

Remind your instructors to keep after your students for solid basic performance of obstacles. Dogs shouldn't be allowed to blow contacts without correction. Nor should they be allowed to miss weave poles without correction. That is not to say that the correction should be harsh or abrupt; a happy but firm correction will do nicely.

Begin your training session by doing the control exercise on page 41 with all students. Then break into groups for the training sets if you're going to work multiple sets simultaneously.

# Week 3: Progress Worksheet

**Instructors:**                                          Date:

| Handler and Dog | Present | Notes |
|---|---|---|
|  |  |  |
|  |  |  |
|  |  |  |
|  |  |  |
|  |  |  |
|  |  |  |
|  |  |  |
|  |  |  |
|  |  |  |
|  |  |  |
|  |  |  |
|  |  |  |

GENERAL NOTES:

# Week 3: Facility Layout

One square = 10'

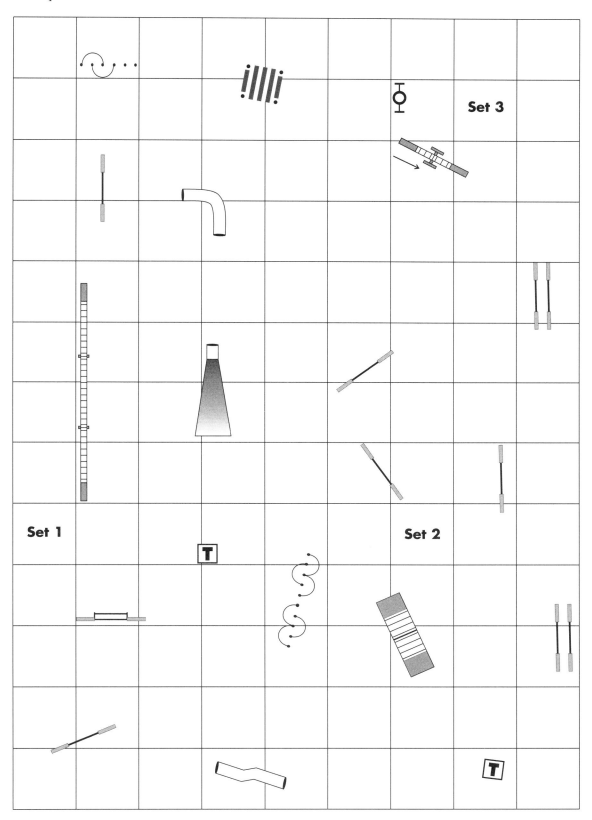

Set 3

Set 1

Set 2

# Week 3: Facility Layout Worksheet

Design your Facility Layout using a 1" = 10' scale (standard agility template)

Advanced Agility Workbook

# Week 3: Exercises

Start the class by doing the control exercise with everyone. Then break into smaller groups if you're going to work the training sets simultaneously.

## Control Exercise

- With all of the dogs on-lead, have your students free heel the dogs in a "follow-the-leader" fashion through the field of equipment. Allow the dogs to sniff and inspect the equipment. Take your time. Let the dogs get any desire to sniff and explore out of their systems.

- Organize your students into two lines, facing one another, about 30' apart.

- Next, have a dog and handler across from each other in either line heel their dogs towards one another so that the handlers meet in the middle (with the dogs on their outside). Instruct the handlers to sit their dogs and extend their right hands for a firm handshake. Then instruct the handlers to down their dogs and remain in the center. Have the next pair of handlers and dogs in line perform the same exercise. By the time all of the dogs and handlers have advanced to the middle and completed their handshake, everyone will be in one long line in the middle with the dogs facing alternately in both directions

- Now instruct your students to walk up and down the line of downed dogs, weaving in and out of them, shaking hands with every other student they meet. If any dog breaks his down, that dog's handler should return to the dog, put the dog back in a down position, and then continue weaving through the line of dogs. Don't spend an excessive amount of time doing this.

- Instruct everyone to return to their dogs.

End of exercise.

## Set 1

Your set consists of four exercises. The first two exercises use the same equipment set as do the last two exercises. No equipment movement will be required.

Your set includes the dogwalk. Remind your students that they should reward their dogs (whether it's with food or with praise) *only* in the contact zone of the descent ramp. The dog is not permitted to leave the contact zone without a quiet release from his handler. If the dog bails off early, he should be picked up and placed back in the contact zone.

Balance your time with each group so that your students get approximately the same amount of work on each of the exercises.

### Working Away

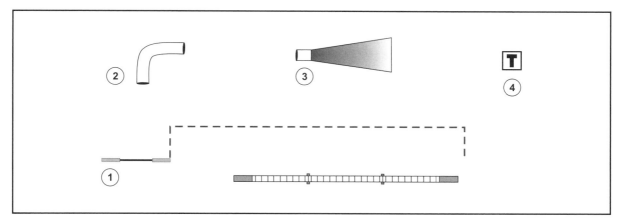

In this exercise you will pattern a sequence that encourages the handler to put more and more working distance between himself and the dog.

Have a baitmaster on hand who will place a food treat on the table for each dog and snatch it away if a dog attempts to skip an obstacle in the sequence.

Follow these steps:

1.  With the dog on his left side, each handler runs the sequence with the dog.

2.  Repeat step 2, but advise the handler to start putting more distance between himself and the dog if the dog shows *any* desire to do the sequence and get at the food treat. The handler does this by gradually hanging back and letting the dog go further ahead of him with each repetition.

3.  Repeat step 3 until the handler is comfortably working behind the line shown in the illustration.

For dogs that are doing really well, tell their handlers that their line is the dogwalk itself. See how they do in this exercise with an obstacle between handler and dog. Consequently, the dogwalk will between dog and handler as the dog runs the sequence.

## Change-Up

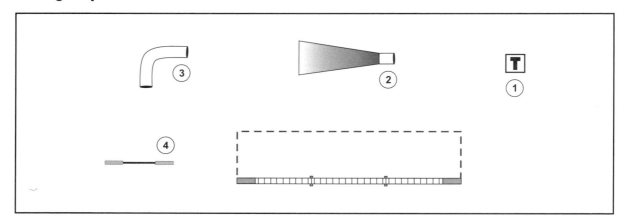

Now, work the set in the opposite direction, reversing the direction of the collapsed tunnel.

Ask your students to start their dogs on the table and then walk *into* the marked handling box before sending the dog to the collapsed tunnel.

Getting the dog into the tunnel may prove to be difficult. The tunnel is away from the handler, and the dog has no motion for the handler to work with. Get your students to experiment with body motion using the area defined by the handling box. Does it help the handler take a step diagonal to the dog before calling the dog off the table? Is movement down and away along the line of the box useful in directing the dog?

Do any of your students have difficulty sending the dog on to the pipe tunnel after the collapsed tunnel?

The handler should attempt to conserve some forward motion as the dog exits from the chute. The handler needs room to take several steps as the dog exits the tunnel and re-orients himself. That motion will be an important signal to the dog to get on and do the pipe tunnel.

Advanced Agility Workbook

## Subtle Deception

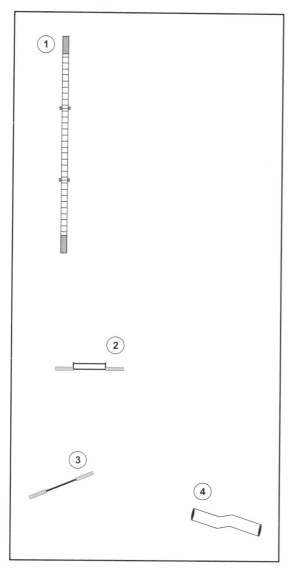

This is the kind of simple and beguiling sequence that troubles even the most advanced handlers in competition. If you draw a line in the illustration from the descent end of the dogwalk over the center of jump #2, you will see that jump #3 is *never* in the dog's field of view. The handler that misses this subtle nuance in competition is doomed to get an off-course or a refusal.

The best handling position for this sequence is probably with the handler working on the outside of the dogwalk (dog on his left). This should pull the dog to the right after jump #2 so that the dog has an opportunity to clearly see jump #3.

If, instead, the handler works the other side of the dogwalk (dog on his right), the dog will veer left as it pushes out over jump #2 and may never even see jump #3. A reliable *Get Out!* command might save the day and allow the handler to push the dog out to jump #3. On the other hand, the dog may get a good enough look at the tunnel that it either takes the off-course or veers left so much that the handler will have to back up the dog for a good approach to #3.

When you set up this exercise in class:

- Don't tell your students about the line-of-sight problem at first and *make* them start with the dog on the right for the first repetition.

- Tell them to really push for speed (as though it were a competition).

Sometimes the best way to get students to behave recklessly (as they would in competition) is to turn the training exercise into a competition. Divide your group into two smaller groups. Tell them that you're going to time each group and the fastest group wins.

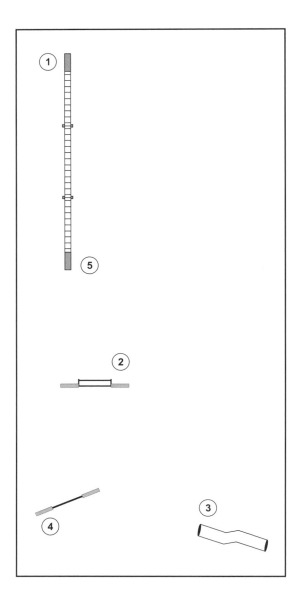

## The Dodge

In this renumbered exercise, you will ask your students to specifically dodge two of the obstacles that were part of the previous sequence. Keeping in mind that the dog may be patterned to the first sequence, the handler will have to get the dog's attention to direct the new sequence.

This new sequence poses an interesting problem for your advanced students. When exiting from a tunnel, a dog will likely turn in the direction on which the handler was working *before* the dog entered the tunnel. Therefore, if the handler starts the sequence with the dog on his right and chooses to cross behind the dog at the pipe tunnel, the dog will likely turn left, the wrong direction, as it exits. This will put the pipe tunnel between the dog and the handler and off-course is possible as the handler attempts to bring the dog back around the front of the tunnel to go to #4.

On the other hand, if the handler chooses to work the dog on his left from the dogwalk and the dog gets even slightly ahead of him, the handler may very well push the dog over the off-course jump at #4. How does a handler resolve this dilemma?

One possibility is for the handler to work the dog on his right for #1–#3 and then hang back by the entrance to the tunnel, rather than trying to cross the dog's path. The dog will turn left out of the tunnel, but this time the handler has a position from which he can push the dog up and out to jump #4 without much difficulty (the dog will be on the handler's left). This solution creates a path for the dog which dodges a potential back-jump of the spread hurdle. This is not a terribly obvious handling solution. Hold back a little while on introducing the possibility in the hopes that it will occur to one of your students.

# Set 2

Your set consists of two exercises. Major equipment movement will be required between exercises. Brief your students immediately that they will be moving the equipment between exercises. You will lay the jump bars on the ground to indicate where to position jumps. Instruct your students to move the jump standards into place.

Your set includes the A-frame. Remind your students that they should reward their dogs (whether it's with food or with praise) *only* in the contact zone of the descent ramp. The dog is not permitted to leave the contact zone without a quiet release from his handler. If the dog bails off early, he should be picked up and placed back in the contact zone.

Your set also includes weave poles. Notice that two of the channel wires have been removed. During the coming weeks, you will continue to remove wires from the chute until only a single wire is left to help with entry.

You will be responsible for running the third part of the eight-week "Raising Jump Heights" program. Be sure to make careful notes of your students' progress so that whoever runs this exercise next week will be properly prepared and can make necessary adjustments.

Balance your time with each group so that your students get approximately the same amount of work on each of the exercises.

## Option Exercises

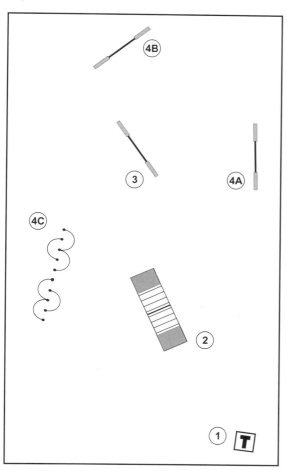

This exercise features three closing options to be performed alternately. The dogs will also get a lot of work on the A-frame. Be sure your students work for the contacts.

**Right turn**—In this first option, turn the dog right after jump #3. Note that jump #4B represents a line-of-sight trap for the dog. The handler should cut sharply right as soon as the dog is committed to jump #3 in order to pull the dog in the correct direction.

**Left turn**—In this option, the handler should boldly push the dog out to jump #4B after jump #3. This really shouldn't be much of a turn. Advise students who turn the sequence into a loopy "S"-shaped exercise to push more boldly for the straight approach.

**Turn back**—In this sequence, the handler has his choice of a right turn or a left turn after jump #3, to get back for the weave poles at #4C. If the handler turns left, the entry to the weave poles will be decidedly cleaner, but the off-course possibility over jump #4B is greater.

There is really no right answer. Your students should use whatever strategy works.

This is a good opportunity to work on handler positioning while the dog is down for the table count, speed on the A-frame, and the entry to the weave poles.

## Raising Jump Heights

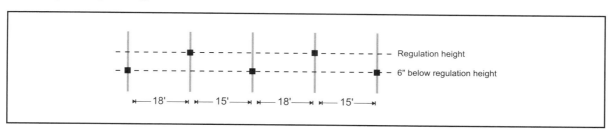

This exercise includes two regulation height jumps in a series of lower jumps. The other jumps in the series are set 6" below the dog's regulation jump height. The jumps are presented to the dog at varied intervals. This spacing is designed to allow the dog to build speed and stride on the approach to the regulation height jumps (the second and fourth jumps).

**NOTE:** For the other exercises this week, the dogs should continue jumping at 6" below their competition height.

Have each dog and handler do at least one repetition of each of the following:

- Leave the dog in a sit-stay behind the first jump, lead out to the third jump, call the dog over the first three jumps, and then complete the sequence running with the dog on the heel-side.

- Leave the dog in a sit-stay behind the first jump, lead out to the third jump, call the dog over the first three jumps, and then complete the sequence running with the dog on the off-side.

- Leave the dog in a sit-stay behind the first jump, lead out past the last jump, and call the dog over all of the entire line of jumps.

**IF A DOG REFUSES THE REGULATION HEIGHT JUMPS:** Back up to the first week of the program, using only one regulation height jump in the sequence.

Keep an eye out for the possibility that the dog may be lame or overweight, or for some other reason does not like jumping regulation height.

If you believe that the dog is fit and healthy and remedies (see the *Intermediate Agility Workbook* for remedial work for jumping problems) aren't working with a particular dog, you might consider recommending that the handler postpone the program to raise the dog's jump height for another month or two. The dog's confidence could certainly be a factor. A dog moving too slowly to gather sufficient momentum to clear the jump, or stopping in front of the jump altogether, is a sign that the dog lacks confidence.

### End Game

Add the table at the end of the line of jumps at least 15' away from the final jump and then have each dog and handler do at least one repetition of each of the previous steps. Set the table at regulation height.

## Set 3

Your set consists of two exercises. Major equipment movement will be required between exercises. Brief your students immediately that they will be moving the equipment between exercises. You will lay the jump bars on the ground to indicate where to position jumps. Instruct your students to move the jump standards into place.

Your set includes the see-saw. Remind your students that they should reward their dogs (whether it's with food or with praise) *only* in the contact zone of the descent ramp. The dog is not permitted to leave the contact zone without a quiet release from his handler. If the dog bails off early, he should be picked up and placed back in the contact zone. You should also be prepared to step in and tip the plank to assist a dog, if necessary.

Your set also includes weave poles. Notice that two of the channel wires have been removed. During the coming weeks, you will continue to remove wires from the chute until only a single wire is left to help with entry.

### Mystery Exercise

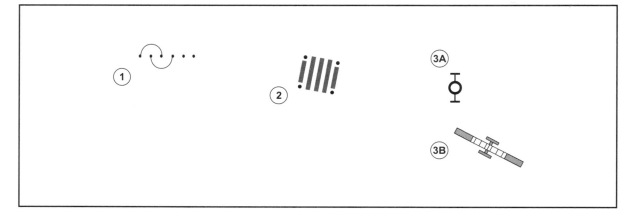

This exercise is specifically designed to tune performance of the key obstacles: weave poles and long jump. It's a thinly veiled *drilling* exercise. Try setting the long jump at the regulation span and see how the dogs do.

The long jump appearing immediately after the weave poles is problematical. It's in the interest of the handler for the dog to get moving at a fast stride in order to clear the span of planks. However, most handlers will pin the dog to their ankle at the weave poles and not be in position to get a lead to draw the dog into a fast stride.

Discuss the following possible solutions to this problem with your students:

- When the dog clears the final pole, run as fast as possible towards the long jump to help the dog build speed.

- Work on a *Go!* command to send the dog running ahead regardless of the handler's speed.

- Leave the dog to complete the weave pole performance and run ahead to get a lead-out advantage.

So, what is the right answer? Clearly, it's whatever the handler can do that actually works. The third option might be the most elegant, but it takes training to be able to work a dog so boldly and it takes a lot of practice for most handlers to trust in the dog that much.

The problem set up by the slow weave poles in sequence with the fast long jump is magnified by the choice of obstacles following the long jump. Alternately have your students take the tire or the see-saw after the long jump. How does this effect each handler's strategy?

If the handler is ahead of the dog at the long jump, directing the dog to the correct closing obstacle should be very manageable. However, what if the handler is behind the dog at the long jump? In this case, the handler's choice of which side to work the dog will influence whether or not the handler is successful in directing the dog to the correct closing obstacle. But what if this handler's dog won't work the poles on the off-side and the handler needs to get the dog to the tire? The options for this dog's handler are getting fewer and fewer. The handler could try starting with the dog on the left, and then sending the dog ahead to do the long jump as he crosses behind the dog and moves towards the tire. Of course, this could be asking for trouble at the long jump because often a dog will shorten stride and slow down if the handler crosses behind.

Keep track of your students' success in this exercise. Encourage them to be bold and to attempt the exercise using different approaches. They'll never know what works and what doesn't work unless they try it! In addition, just because one solution works doesn't mean that the handler should stop trying other options; there may be one that works even better.

## Recall Exercises

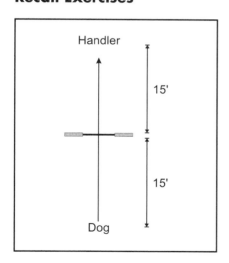

These exercises were developed by Nancy Gyes of California. In addition to using these exercises in class, you will find that these are good exercises to give for homework since they do not require much equipment and the student can gradually increase the level of difficulty.

Have the handler leave his dog 15' from the jump and lead out 15' on the other side of the jump as shown in the illustration on the left. The handler should then call the dog over the jump.

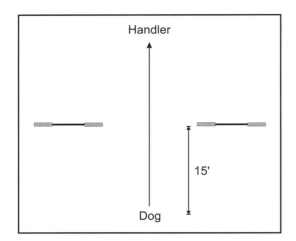

If you are giving this exercise to students for homework, instruct your students to continue increasing the distance between the dog and the jump and the handler and the jump until both dog and handler can be up to 30' from the jump without the dog running around or under the jump.

For this exercise, place two winged jumps side-by-side and 15' apart. Have the handler leave the dog 15' behind the jumps and then lead out 15' beyond the jumps as shown in the illustration on the left. The handler should then call the dog *between* the jumps using a specific "front" type of command.

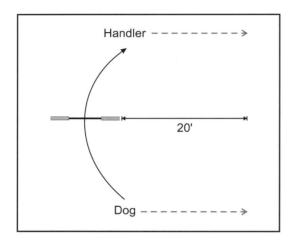

If the dog wants to take a jump rather than come between the jumps, the handler should position the dog closer to the jumps but lead out to the same position.

If you are giving this exercise to students for homework, instruct your students to gradually decrease the distance between the jumps.

Have the handler leave the dog 15' behind the jump, and slightly off-center to the jump, as shown in the illustration on the left. The handler should lead out 15' beyond the jump and position himself perpendicular to the dog as shown. The handler then calls the dog and uses a hand signal to direct the dog over the jump.

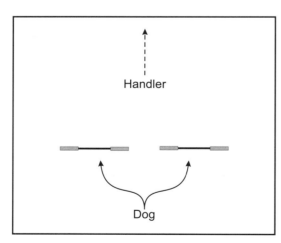

If you are giving this exercise to students for homework, instruct your students to gradually move both the handler's starting position and the dog's starting position laterally, until both handler and dog can start the exercise 20' out to the side of the jump as shown.

For this exercise, place two winged jumps side-by-side and 5' apart. Have the handler leave the dog 10' behind the jumps and then lead out to a position that's 10' beyond the jumps as shown in the illustration on the left. The handler should use a hand signal to direct the dog first over one jump and then the other.

If you are giving this exercise to students for homework, instruct your students to gradually increase the distance between the jumps up to 20'. The handler can also increase the difficulty of the exercise by increasing his starting distance from the jumps to 20'. Continue to leave the dog 10' behind the jumps.

# Week 3: Student Notes

By now, you are familiar with the directional commands *Come!*, *Go!*, and *Get Out!* (and hopefully so is your dog!). Some handlers also find it useful to teach their dogs the directional commands *Left!* and *Right!*. Because these commands are used to direct the dog relative to *the dog's* position and not the handler's (for example, *Left!* means the dog should turn to *his* left, not yours), many people find them difficult to use effectively. While it's easy when both you and your dog are facing the same direction, it's more of a challenge to give the correct command when the dog is facing you. Despite this fact, these commands can be very useful if you are going to be competing in gamblers classes, and also if you tend to be much slower than your dog since they give you a way to direct the dog when you may be out of position.

*Artist: Nancy Krouse-Culley*

There are a number of effective ways to teach directional commands such as *Left!*, *Right!*, and *Go On!* to a dog. The following is a "no frills" program for getting started on teaching these commands. The program is different depending on whether your dog is more toy motivated or food motivated.

## Starting to Teach Directionals: Toy-Motivated Dog

The first step is to find a throwable object that your dog really covets—such as a Frisbee™, tennis ball, or a tug toy. Pack up your toy of choice and your dog and go find a good-sized open area (a baseball field, for example). If your dog does not have a reliable recall, bring along a 20' lightweight long line for this exercise.

1. With the dog off-leash (unless you are working on the long line), put him on a sit-stay in heel position.

2. Throw the toy out about 30' *straight* ahead of you.

   **NOTE:** If your dog is not reliable on a stay, hold him by the collar while you throw the toy. If the dog attempts to get up or lunge forward for the toy, give him a gentle collar check and place him back in a sit without comment. Once the dog is sitting and is *not* pulling at his collar, you can release him for the ball as described in the next step. Holding the collar should only be necessary for the first few repetitions. You want the dog to stay on his own so that you can use your hand to give a hand signal rather than holding back the dog.

3. Using both a hand signal (use the hand closest to the dog) and a verbal command such as *Go On!*, tell the dog to go out after his toy.

   **NOTE:** If the dog doesn't get up and go after the toy, encourage him a bit. You may even want to gently help him out of his sit and repeat the command. Some dogs are initially reluctant to break the stay without an "official" release command. These dogs will learn that it's okay to follow another command at this point.

4. Praise the dog and play with him a bit when he brings his toy back.

5. Set up again and repeat the exercise. Always be sure that you use the *same* verbal command and the *same* visual signal. Consistency is very important.

6. Once the dog is comfortable going out for the toy (that is, he shows no hesitation at all when commanded), try the exercise with the dog on a sit-stay on your right side.

Practice this exercise 10 minutes every day for a week. Every now and then change the area of the field where you working and work in the oppositie direction (for example, if you are facing North when you try this exercise then try it facing South). Now start introducing a new command—either *Left!* or *Right!*.

1. With the dog off-leash (unless you are working on the long line), put him on a sit-stay in heel position.

2. Throw the toy out about 30' to your left. Make sure that you have the dog's attention before you throw the toy so he sees which way it's going.

3. Using both a hand signal (use the hand closest to the dog) and a verbal command such as *Left!*, tell the dog to go out after his toy.

   **NOTE:** When introducing this new command, if the dog doesn't get up and go after the toy, encourage him.

4. Praise the dog and play with him a bit.

5. Set up again and repeat the exercise. Again, always be sure that you use the same verbal command and the same visual signal.

6. Once the dog is comfortable going out for the toy (that is, he shows no hesitation when commanded), try the exercise with the dog on a sit-stay on your right side.

7. Every now and then throw the toy straight ahead and practice your *Go On!* command.

Practice this for up to 10 minutes every day for a week. Again, vary the area of the field where you work or try going to a *different* place to practice.

The next week, repeat the previous steps to introduce your dog to the *Right!* command. Remember to continue practicing your *Left!* and *Go On!* commands.

**NOTE:** If at any time during training the dog breaks the sit-stay, go get him and the toy. Bring the dog back to his original position and put him in a sit without comment. Start the exercise again.

Once the dog is comfortable with all three directionals, you can stop placing the dog in a sit-stay to start the exercise. Instead, allow the dog to start the exercise from a free position. It's okay if he's not right next to you or even if he's not facing the same direction as you are— just make sure that you give him the correct command for the direction that he is *facing* when you throw the ball. Remember, when you command *Left!*, you want the dog turning to *his* left!

After a couple months of playing this game (sooner for some dogs), you can change the rules a bit to make the dog really think about this! Command the dog to *Go On!* but do *not* throw the toy straight ahead. As the dog is moving away from you, throw the toy to his right (only about 10' away) and give him a *Right!* command *and* a right signal. Give the signal even if the dog is not looking at you and hold that signal—since once the dog realizes the toy is not out there, he will look to you for direction and you want him to get used to going in the direction that you're pointing. If the dog is confused, help him find the toy.

## Starting to Teach Directionals: Food-Motivated Dog

Some dogs don't care about toys (although many of these dogs just haven't been introduced to the *right* toy yet). Since throwing food on the ground in training is not good practice, you can make an attractive throwable object for these chowhounds using a piece of clear plastic tubing, a 35mm film cannister, a whiffle ball, a very small Tupperware™ container, or any object that you can poke holes in so that the dog can see and/or smell the food but not be able to get it without your intervention.

Using such a training aid, you can teach directional commands to the dog using the method previously described for the toy-motivated dog. However, first make sure you teach the dog that this object is an interesting thing to chase and ideally to bring back to you. If the dog will not bring the object back to you, make sure that you follow after the dog and get him a food reward from the "holder" when he does the exercise correctly. Do *not* allow the dog to play with the food container or make it available to him outside of training since most dogs will take the opportunity to destroy the container and eat it as well as the treats!

You can also start teaching directionals to food-motivated dogs using a stationary target method. This method requires more set up on your part for each repetition (unless you have a child, friend, or neighbor who will help you out); however, the handler does not have to actually go out to give the reward to the dog.

You will need four *identical* targets. A good target must be clearly visible to the dog in the grass and you must be able to leave a piece of food on the top of the target without it falling off. Good targets for this exercise are the white plastic ice buckets found at hotels or the large plastic buckets that the potato salad comes in at the grocery store. You just put them on the ground upside down and you have a great target.

Pack up your targets, your food treat of choice, and your dog and find a good-sized open area (a baseball field, for example). If your dog does not have a reliable recall, bring along a 20' lightweight long line for this exercise.

Set up your four targets in a baseball-diamond configuration as shown in the illustration on the left. There should be approximately 60' between the "top" and "bottom" target as well as the "left" and "right" target.

1.  Place a treat (just a small piece) on one of the targets—it doesn't matter which target you use. Let the dog see you (or your assistant) baiting the target.

2.  With the dog off-leash (unless you are working on the long line), go to the center of the "diamond" and put the dog on a sit-stay in heel position. You and the dog should be facing the target that you baited.

3.  Using both a hand signal (use the hand closest to the dog) and a verbal command such as *Go On!*, tell the dog to go out and get the treat.

    **NOTE:** If the dog doesn't get up and go after the food, encourage him a bit. You may even want to gently help him out of his sit and repeat the *Go On!* command. Some dogs are initially reluctant to break the stay without an "official" release command. These dogs will learn that it's okay to follow another command at this point.

4.  Praise the dog.

5.  Call the dog back to you. Set up again and repeat the exercise. Always be sure to use the same verbal command and the same visual signal.

6.  Once the dog is comfortable going out for the treat (that is, he shows no hesitation when commanded), try the exercise with the dog on a sit-stay on your right side.

Practice this 10 minutes every day for a week. Rotate which target you choose to bait, but you and the dog should always be facing toward the target you baited. For example, if you bait the "top" target on one repetition then bait the "bottom" target on the next repetition so that the dog will be working the *Go On!* moving in a different direction. After the week is over, start introducing a new command—either *Left!* or *Right!*.

1.  Place a treat on one of the targets.

2.  With the dog off-leash (unless you are working on the long line), go to the center of the "diamond" and put the dog on a sit-stay in heel position. You should be facing the target *to the right* of the one you baited so the dog will have to go left to get the treat.

    **NOTE:** Make sure that you have the dog's attention before you start because he will probably be focusing on the target that's straight ahead of you.

3.  Using both a hand signal (use the hand closest to the dog) and a verbal command such as *Left!*, tell the dog to go out after the treat.

    **NOTE:** If the dog goes to the wrong target, do not allow him to wander and sniff—the point of the exercise is not for the dog to find the correct target by trial and error, but for him to learn that the verbal and non-verbal directional signals you give him will direct him to the correct target. Bring the dog back to his original position and put him in a sit without comment. Start the exercise again.

4.  Praise the dog.

5.  Call the dog back to you. Set up again and repeat the exercise. Always be sure to use *the same* verbal command and the same visual signal.

6. Once the dog is comfortable going out for the treat (that is, he shows no hesitation when commanded), try the exercise with the dog on a sit-stay on your right side.

7. Every now and then send the dog straight ahead to a baited target so that you also practice your *Go On!* command.

Practice this for up to 10 minutes every day for a week. Again, vary which target you bait. You may also want to try going to a different place to practice.

The next week, repeat the previous steps to introduce your dog to the *Right!* command. Remember to continue practicing your *Left!* and *Go On!*.

**NOTE:** If at any time during training the dog breaks the sit-stay, go and get him. Do not let him get the food (you may have to move pretty fast). If you can't stop the dog from getting the food, then you need an assistant to help you or a long line. Bring the dog back to his original position and put him in a sit without comment. Start the exercise again.

Once the dog is comfortable with all three directionals, you can stop putting the dog on a sit-stay to start the exercise. Allow him to start the exercise from a free position. It's okay if he's not right next you—just make sure that he's facing the same way that you are so the directionals are correct and so that you're sending him toward a baited target!

At this point in the training, it is desirable to bait the target without the dog seeing you do it if at all possible. This is where you really need a helper. You turn the dog away from your working area and let the helper bait one of the targets. The helper should then move to neutral position so that he doesn't influence which target the dog chooses. You then set up for the directional you want to practice. The dog learns that there may be a reward on a target even if he doesn't see you put one there...and, if he doesn't go the direction you tell him to there is no reward to be found!

After a couple months of playing this game (sooner for some dogs), you can change the rules a bit to make the dog really think about this. For example, command the dog to *Go On!* towards a target that is *not* baited. As the dog is moving away from you, give him either a *Right!* or *Left!* command *and* an appropriate hand signal to send him to a target that *is* baited. Give the signal even if the dog is not looking at you and hold that signal. Once the dog realizes the target is not baited, he will look to you for direction and you want him to get used to going in the direction that you're pointing. If the dog is confused, help him find the correct target. Only one target is ever baited in this game.

# Week 4: Instructor Notes

What does a handler mean when he tells his dog *Hurry!*? Sure, *we* know that it means go faster. But what does the dog think it means?

You can actually put this to a scientific test. Ask the handler to demonstrate what *Hurry!* means on the flat, away from the equipment. Chances are the handler has never taught the dog what it means and the command has absolutely no effect on or away from the equipment.

So, your advice to the handler who uses *Hurry!* or *Hurry Up!* to nag his dog around the course, is to stop it unless the dog is in a specific program to learn what the command means.

*Artist: Jo Ann Mather*

The dog's lack of speed might be a function of confidence. If the dog isn't sure whether he is doing right, wondering what the handler wants, he may work tentatively. This is frequently the case with novice dogs. For these dogs the handler must be urged to patience. As the dog's confidence grows, so will the speed. A dog that barely makes it through a novice class in course time may one day be blowing out course time in the advanced classes by ten or fifteen seconds. This is a common phenomenon.

The dog's lack of speed also might be a function of the handler's speed. A handler who is exceptionally slow does not inspire a dog to move faster. This is worth pointing out to handlers who are intentionally moving slow. They aren't doing their dogs any favor by waiting around. The handler should get ahead of the dog as fast as he can and make the dog move at the speed he is capable in order to catch up.

|  | Set 1 | Set 2 | Set 3 |
|---|---|---|---|
| **Week 4** | **Playground and Playground Option** *Obstacles:* A-frame, two pipe tunnels, four winged jumps, tire | **Ken's Innovation and On the Other Hand** *Obstacles:* see-saw, three winged jumps | **Raising Jump Heights and End Game** *Obstacles:* five winged jumps, table |

**NOTE:** This week you are going to do a group exercise at the end of class. For the group exercise, the obstacles required will be: dogwalk, see-saw, A-frame, tire, pipe tunnel, weave poles, and four winged jumps.

## Organizational Notes

Review the progress notes from Week 3. Ask your instructors if the exercises for Week 3 were too hard or too easy for the class. If so, should today's exercises be modified in any way? Make note of any modifications to exercises in your master workbook. These notes will provide valuable intelligence for future classes. Devise a plan for doing remedial work with dogs or handlers whose problems may cause delays in today's training plan.

Begin your training session by doing the control exercise on page 57 with all students. Then break into groups for the training sets if you're going to work multiple sets simultaneously.

Make sure to save about half of your class time for the group exercise "Silent Running" on page 60. Note that the transition from the regular exercises to the group exercise requires a considerable movement of obstacles. When you gather your students together for regular housekeeping announcements and so forth, you need to prepare them to help with the task of reassembling the field. Tell them to be prepared to put their dogs away and help move equipment about halfway through the class.

# Week 4: Progress Worksheet

**Instructors:**                                                **Date:**

| Handler and Dog | Present | Notes |
|---|---|---|
|  |  |  |
|  |  |  |
|  |  |  |
|  |  |  |
|  |  |  |
|  |  |  |
|  |  |  |
|  |  |  |
|  |  |  |
|  |  |  |
|  |  |  |
|  |  |  |

GENERAL NOTES:

# Week 4: Facility Layout

One square = 10'

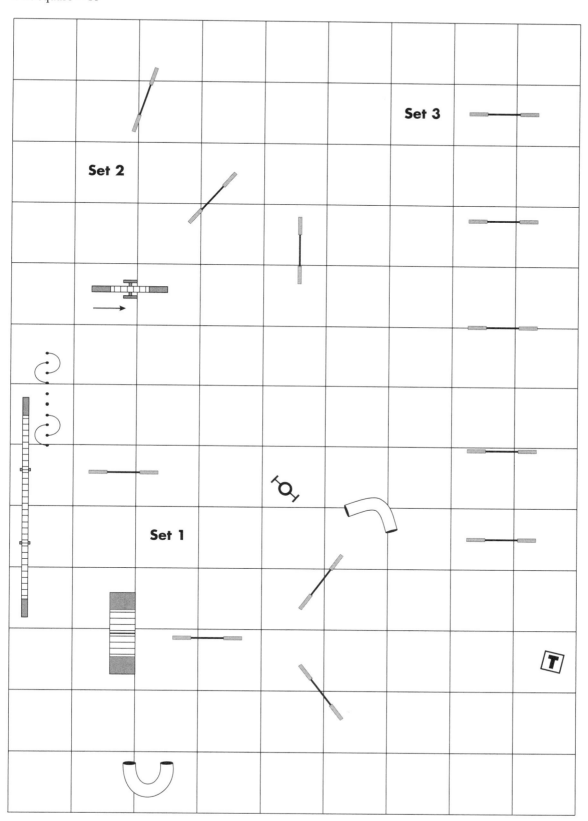

# Week 4: Facility Layout Worksheet

Design your Facility Layout using a 1" = 10' scale (standard agility template)

# Week 4: Exercises

Start the class by doing the control exercise with everyone. Then break into smaller groups if you're going to work the training sets simultaneously.

## Control Exercise

- With all of the dogs on-lead, have your students free heel the dogs in a "follow-the-leader" fashion through the field of equipment. Allow the dogs to sniff and inspect the equipment. Take your time. Let the dogs get any desire to sniff and explore out of their systems.

- Instruct your students that you will now do an attention exercise. The purpose of the exercise is to work on the *Come!* command with a bit of motivation added using the leash. Have everyone free heel their dogs on-lead simultaneously, but individually rather than in a follow-the-leader queue. About every ten seconds each handler should unexpectedly change direction, giving the dog a *Come!* command. If the dog doesn't immediately change direction to match the handler's new direction, the handler should give a crisp "pop" on the leash to remind the dog that the *Come!* is not optional. Tell your students that the ideal moment to change direction and command the dog to *Come!* is when the dog is approaching an obstacle or another dog.

End of exercise.

## Set 1

Your set consists of two exercises that use the same equipment set up. No equipment movement will be required. You will just need to renumber the sequence.

Your set includes the A-frame. Remind your students that they should reward their dogs (whether it's with food or with praise) *only* in the contact zone of the descent ramp. The dog is not permitted to leave the contact zone without a quiet release from his handler. If the dog bails off early, he should be picked up and placed back in the contact zone.

### Playground

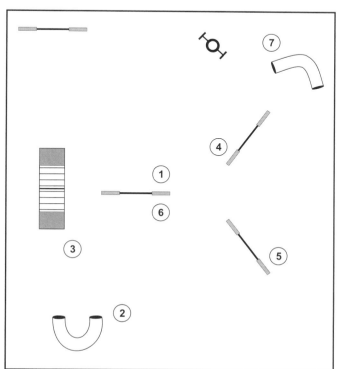

This exercise, which was designed by Stuart Mah of California, will test your students' handling abilities as they avoid the numerous off-course possibilities surrounding the numbered sequence. At the center of the set is a pinwheel which doesn't itself present a high degree of difficulty. However, the handler must be aware of his position when setting up for the pinwheel, or when leaving it.

When the dog exits the A-frame is the dog on the handler's left side? If so, the dog is going to be presented with the off-course jump, the tire, and the tunnel (#7) during the transition to #4. This is no problem if the handler can reliably turn his dog to jump #4 or if the dog is very slow. However, you might recommend that a better solution would be for the handler get in front of the dog at the A-frame and counter-rotate (turn right towards the dog) to put the dog on his right side. The handler would then push the dog over #4 and cross behind to head into the pinwheel.

## Playground Option

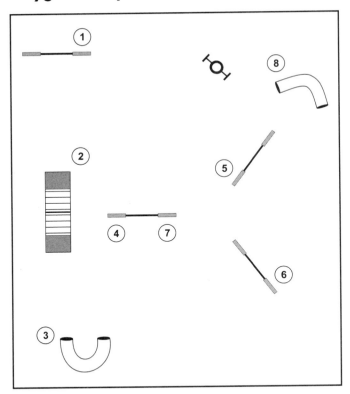

This renumbered exercise provides your advanced students some new challenges. How do they handle the additional change of sides?

Do they recognize the lure of the pipe tunnel after the A-frame and the potential for a missed contact? The handler is going to have to work hard to get the dog to concentrate on the down-side contact and not the tunnel.

Handlers that execute a change of sides while the dog is in the pipe tunnel at #3 (blind cross) to put the dog on their left side to head into the pinwheel may have the most successful results in this exercise.

# Set 2

Your set consists of two exercises that use the same equipment set up. No equipment movement will be required. You will just need to renumber the sequence.

Your set includes the see-saw. Remind your students that they should reward their dogs (whether it's with food or with praise) *only* in the contact zone of the descent ramp. The dog is not permitted to leave the contact zone without a quiet release from his handler. If the dog bails off early, he should be picked up and placed back in the contact zone.

## Ken's Innovation

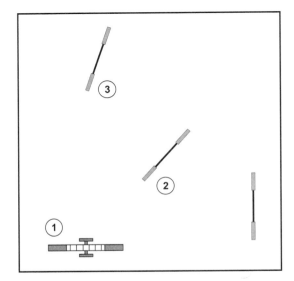

Here's something that your students can expect to see in competition. The handler is required to push the dog into a perilous "pocket" and then turn the dog in a new direction to get out of the pocket.

If the handler pushes too hard/too far in trying to get the dog lined up for jump #2, the dog is likely to commit over the off-course jump. However, if the handler hangs back too much, the dog might very well cross *back* over the plane of jump #2, without ever seeing the jump, and earn the refusal.

The handling of this set is a personal matter that must be worked out between dog and handler.

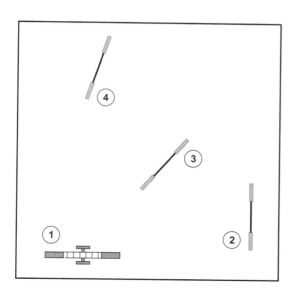

## On the Other Hand

In this renumbered exercise, the handler is required to turn the dog after jump #2. Which is the best direction for the dog to turn in order to make the transition to #3?

A right turn after #2 lines up the dog for a straighter path between #3 and #4. A left turn provides a shorter overall path for the dog. Which is best?

There is no right answer. Whatever works. Encourage your students to try both options.

# Set 3

You will be responsible for running the fourth part of the eight-week "Raising Jump Heights" program. Be sure to make careful notes of your students' progress so that whoever runs this exercise next week will be properly prepared and can make necessary adjustments.

## Raising Jump Heights

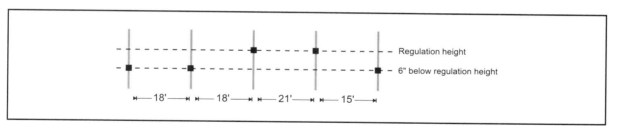

This exercise includes two regulation height jumps in a series of lower jumps. The other jumps in the series are set 6" below the dog's regulation jump height. The jumps are presented to the dog at varied intervals. This spacing is designed to allow the dog to build speed and stride on the approach to the regulation height jumps (the third and fourth jumps).

**NOTE:** For the other exercises this week, the dogs should continue jumping at 6" below their competition height.

Have each dog and handler do at least one repetition of each of the following:

• Leave the dog in a sit-stay behind the first jump, lead out to the third jump, call the dog over the first three jumps, and then complete the sequence running with the dog on the heel-side.

• Leave the dog in a sit-stay behind the first jump, lead out to the third jump, call the dog over the first three jumps, and then complete the sequence running with the dog on the off-side.

• Leave the dog in a sit-stay behind the first jump, lead out past the last jump, and call the dog over all of the entire line of jumps.

**IF A DOG REFUSES THE REGULATION HEIGHT JUMPS:** Back up to Week 3 of the program.

## End Game

Add the table at the end of the line of jumps at least 15' away from the final jump and then have each dog and handler do at least one repetition of each of the previous steps. Set the table at regulation height.

# Group Exercise: Silent Running

After you have finished the regular exercises for this week, gather all of your instructors and students together and reset the field for the group exercise. You should try to reserve about half of your class time for this exercise.

This set includes the A-frame, dogwalk, *and* see-saw. Although there will be many things for the handlers to think about in this set, remind your students that they still need to be attentive to working *all* of the contacts. The set also includes the weave poles. Notice that two more of the channel wires have been removed.

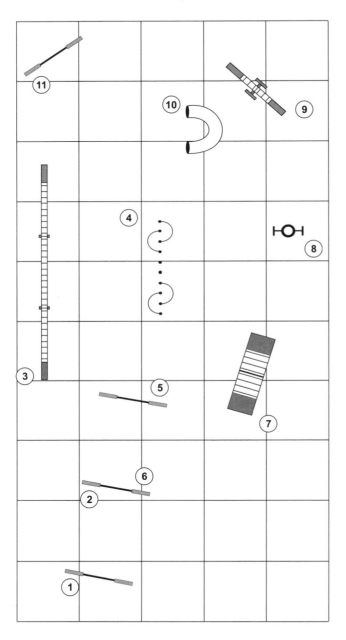

Brief your students that during this exercise they will *not* be allowed to talk to their dogs, clap their hands, or stomp their feet on the ground, with the following exceptions: 1) they may give the dog one command to start the exercise; and 2) they may give a quiet release from the contacts.

The purpose of this exercise is to explore the possibilities of communicating with a dog by non-verbal means. The value of the exercise is to make the handler understand what role body position and hand signals play in communicating flow to the dog. This is *not* to recommend this as a method for working the dog in competition.

Do not allow handlers to lead out. How does the handler communicate the turn after jump #2 to the dogwalk? If the handler starts with the dog on his right, he can hang back and move laterally left as the dog commits to jump #2. The dog should pull to the left and look back to the handler, at which point the handler should give a hand signal to the dogwalk. Once the dog has committed to the up ramp, the handler can cross behind the dog to put the dog on his left.

How does the handler negotiate the dog past the off-course perils from the dog walk to the weave poles at #4? Working the dog on his left down the dogwalk, the handler can counter-rotate as the dog dismounts, putting the dog on his right, and then give the dog a signal to the weave poles.

How on earth will the handler get the dog to enter the weave poles and continue through them to the end without making a sound? Maybe it can't be done. But, insist anyway. Remind the handler that he may use only his body. Work for an upright posture. The handler may learn something about his dog's ability to weave that he didn't know before.

How will the handler turn the dog from jump #6, 180° to the A-frame? If the handler worked the dog on his right through the weave poles, the handler can hang back and move laterally left as the dog commits to jump #6. When the dog pulls to the left and looks back, the handler should then give a signal to the A-frame.

Some handlers rely on a *Wait!* or *Easy!* command when their dog performs the see-saw. What should they do in this exercise? Shut up and dance. It's probably time the handler trusted his dog to figure out the see-saw.

Advanced Agility Workbook

# Week 4: Student Notes

Many handlers resort to using a *Hurry!* command to try to speed up a dog's performance. If you're one of these handlers, can you explain exactly what *Hurry!* means to your dog, and more importantly, can you demonstrate the command on the flat away from the obstacles? Did you ever specifically train a *Hurry!* command so that the dog knows what you want?

*Artist: Nancy Krouse-Culley*

Instead of using *Hurry!*, try using the word *Go!* since you have been doing training with this word both in class and at home. Remember, *Go!* tells the dog to move ahead in the direction that he is going. With a little bit of work at home, you can enhance your dog's reaction to the *Go!* command. The goal should be that if you say *Go! Go! Go!* in an excited voice to urge your dog to greater speed on the agility field, it will naturally kick an internal drive into gear because the dog associates *Go!* with positive things.

An easy way to work on the Go! command is to quarter your dog's evening meal, with the intention of using it as incentive for the dog. Put one quarter of the food in the dog's dish. Take the dog about 15' away from the dish, aim the dog at the dish, hold him by the hips so that he's straining to get away from you and go to the dish, and then release him. As the dog runs to the dish, yell *Go go go!* in an excited voice. After doing this a few weeks, you can put a jump between the dog and the dish and do the same exercise.

## Problem Weave Pole Entries

In competition, weave poles are not always presented in a nice, smooth straight-line flow. In fact, you'll find that some judges relish giving you problem entries to the weave poles.

The problem entry has many ways to manifest itself. This exercise emphasizes performance of the weave poles after a 180° turn. In the illustration on the left, you can see that with your dog on the heel side, you will simply pivot around and use a strong *Come!* command to turn your dog to follow you.

You can do the same thing with the dog on your right side as shown in the middle illustration.

The illustration on the right, however, shows a fancy handling maneuver that allows you to make the 180° turn and switch to working your dog on your left side for performance of the weave poles.

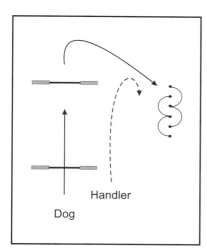

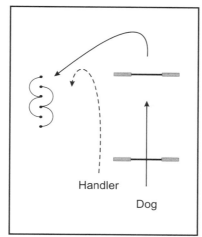

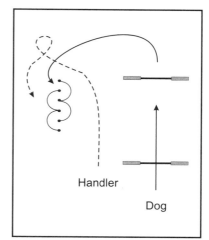

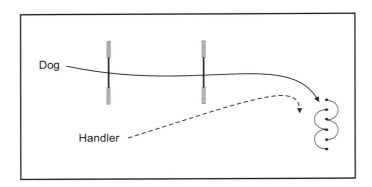

Some judges seem to relish making the weave poles an object of ugly possibilities. In the illustration on the left, you can see a fast flow to a "depressed" or flat angle entry to the weave poles. This really isn't all that tough. You can see that the handler pushes up just hard enough to kick the dog out just a bit. Then the handler turns sharply, calling his dog after him.

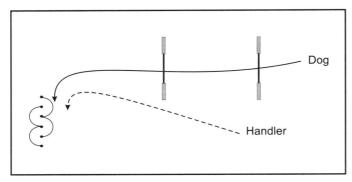

But oh my! Look what happens when you are faced with the mirror image of the same sequence. You have your dog on the right side and the dog's path is longer because he has to wrap around the first pole to make a correct entry. In this illustration, you can see that an attempt to bump the dog out falls short and the dog misses the entry. How else could you try to handle this set up?

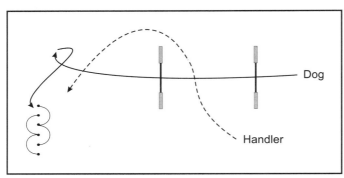

The illustration on the left shows the handler being very thoughtful and purposeful in the attack on this weave pole performance. The handler crosses up behind the dog as the dog commits over the second jump. Consequently, the dog turns right—*away* from the weave poles. Then the handler neatly changes direction and the dog turns with him. This slick maneuver allows the dog a straight on approach to the poles.

# Week 5: Instructor Notes

There's a persistent intelligence out in the world that if you want to be competitive, you can't do both agility and obedience at the same time. You'll hear similar warnings about flyball, lure coursing, herding, and any other dog sport you can imagine. This is partly nonsense.

Susan Garrett won the 24" division of the USDAA® Nationals in July of 1996 with a Border Collie named Stoni (OTCH/FBCh McCann Estonia). Two weeks later, she and Stoni took second place in the 25th Annual World Series Tournament Top Dog competition, an obedience competition. This is also a dog that was a member of the 1992, 1993, and 1994 American Flyball Championship teams and has placed highly in herding trials.

*Artist: Rebecca Cheek*

On the other hand, excellence in multiple dog sports is earned only by an incredible commitment to being the very best, coupled with an uncanny knowledge of what path must be traveled to arrive there. So the advice to a handler to quit agility because it's "ruining" the obedience team might be right advice in some cases. It might serve the handler and dog to get to work, get focused, and avoid distractions. However, if a handler has only a thimble's worth of attention, it seems a shame to waste it on an obedience career that is surely doomed from the beginning. The right advice in this case might be to quit obedience for agility, which at least has the saving grace of being fun!

So agility instructor, you'll have an opportunity from time to time to give one of these directionless individuals a bit of advice that will change their lives.

| | Set 1 | Set 2 | Set 3 |
|---|---|---|---|
| **Week 5** | **Weave 'n the Wheel Exercises**<br>*Obstacles:* five winged jumps and two short sets of weave poles<br><br>*Note:* Minor equipment movement is required between exercises. | **Run Around Sue and Run Around Sue Variation**<br>*Obstacles:* one winged jump, tire, dogwalk, pipe tunnel, double spread hurdle<br><br>**Off-Side Sweep**<br>*Obstacles:* A-frame, two nonwinged jumps<br><br>*Note:* Minor equipment movement is required between exercises. | **In Front**<br>*Obstacles:* see-saw, table, four winged jumps<br><br>**Raising Jump Heights and End Game**<br>*Obstacles:* five winged jumps, long jump, table<br><br>*Note:* Major equipment movement is required between exercises. |

## Organizational Notes

Review with all instructors the notes from the Week 4 Progress Worksheets. Discuss how you will divide up your class this week. You might consider grouping dogs with similar problems.

Begin your training session by doing the control exercise on page 67 with all students. Then break into groups for the training sets if you're going to work multiple sets simultaneously.

# Week 5: Progress Worksheet

**Instructors:**                                                    **Date:**

| Handler and Dog | Present | Notes |
|---|---|---|
|  |  |  |
|  |  |  |
|  |  |  |
|  |  |  |
|  |  |  |
|  |  |  |
|  |  |  |
|  |  |  |
|  |  |  |
|  |  |  |
|  |  |  |
|  |  |  |

GENERAL NOTES:

# Week 5: Facility Layout

One square = 10'

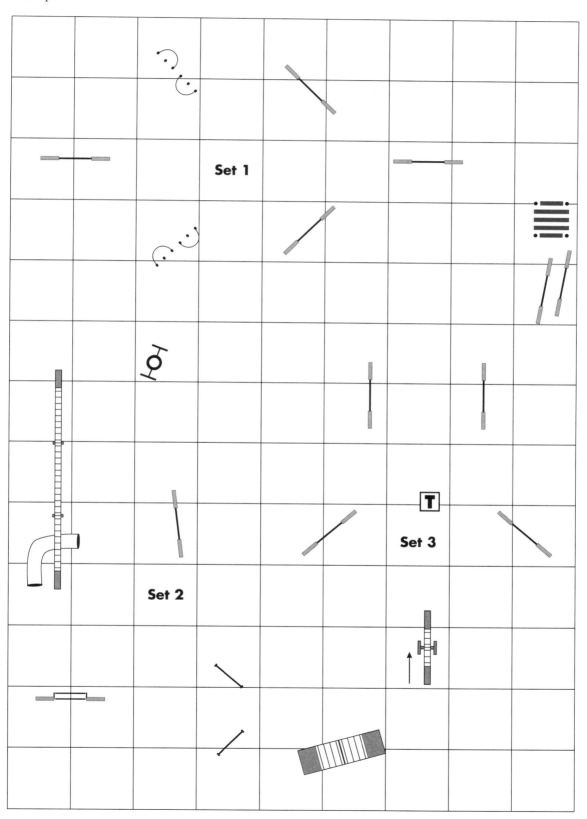

# Week 5: Facility Layout Worksheet

Design your Facility Layout using a 1" = 10' scale (standard agility template)

# Week 5: Exercises

Start the class by doing the control exercise with everyone. Then break into smaller groups if you're going to work the training sets simultaneously.

## Control Exercise

- With all of the dogs *off-leash*, have your students free heel the dogs in a "follow-the-leader" fashion through the field of equipment. Allow the dogs to sniff and inspect the equipment. Take your time. Let the dogs get any desire to sniff and explore out of their systems.

- Instruct your students to heel the dogs at attention into a long line. You need 8' to 10' between dogs.

- Have your students leave the dogs in a down-stay and walk as far away from their dogs as they are comfortable. Whether that's across the field, or just a few feet away, is entirely up to the owner.

- Recall the dogs *one* at a time. Each handler commands his dog to *Come!*. With any luck, the right dog will get up and come directly to the handler. If the dog does not do so, the handler will go and collect his dog. If the wrong dog comes, that dog's handler will collect his dog and put him back in a down with the other dogs.

- Praise and hold on to the dog until everyone has recalled their dogs.

End of exercise.

## Set 1

Your set consists of seven exercises that use the same equipment set. However, minor equipment movement will be required between the fourth and fifth exercises. Brief your students immediately that they will be moving the equipment between exercises. You will lay the jump bars on the ground to indicate where to position jumps. Instruct your students to move the jump standards into place.

Balance your time with each group so that your students get approximately the same amount of work on each of the exercises.

### Weave 'n the Wheel

These exercises are designed to allow your students to practice weave pole entries off a curve. You will renumber the set a number of times to vary the challenge from repetition to repetition.

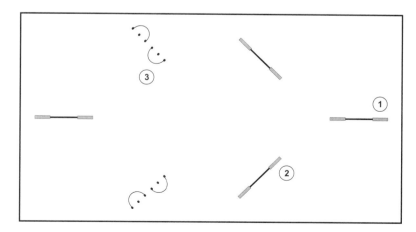

In this first exercise, the dog takes a simple turn for a direct entry to the poles. However, the long transitional distance will give some dogs problems. Do *not* allow a lead-out.

Handlers will be inclined to start with the dog on the left. Let them run the sequence once this way, but also ask your students to do one repetition with the dog on the right.

A right-sided start will require the handler to push the dog over jump #2, and then cross behind.

Do you see a difference in the dog's speed or the tightness of the turn based on which side the dog works?

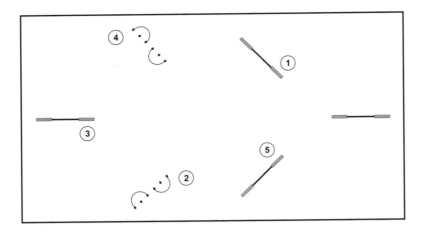

The difficulty in this exercise will be the entry to the weave poles at #4. If the handler allows the dog to turn too abruptly after jump #3, a refusal or ugly entry is possible.

The handler's job is to push the dog out and away after jump #3 until he's lined up for a smooth entry.

Do two repetitions of this sequence. Do *not* allow a lead-out.

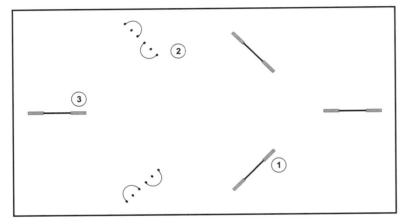

This approach to the weave poles will be a challenge for handlers with dogs that will not weave on right.

Do *not* allow a lead-out. Do one repetition with the dog starting on the handler's left, and one with the dog starting on the handler's right.

When starting with the dog on his left, the handler will either have to cross behind at the beginning of the poles, or "head" the dog at the end of the poles to the final jump.

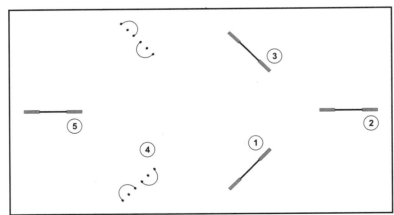

This exercise combines some of the handling problems of the previous sequences.

Do *not* allow a lead-out. Do two repetitions of this exercise. See what side handlers choose to start the dog on.

If starting with the dog on his right, the handler can take the comfortable inside pocket of the pinwheel. The handler can either cross in front of the dog before the weave poles, or "head" the dog to the final jump after the weave poles.

If starting with the dog on his left, the handler is going to have to run around the outside of the pinwheel (that's a long way) or immediately cross behind the dog to get the dog to jump #2.

Advanced Agility Workbook

WEEK 5

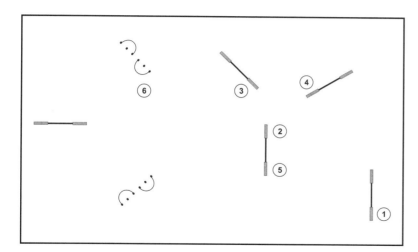

For this exercise, you will need to move the equipment and add another jump. This makes the wheel considerably tighter and even more challenging for your students.

Do *not* allow a lead-out. Allow your students to do two repetitions of the exercise.

You will find that the handler can comfortably work his dog on the heel-side for the entire sequence.

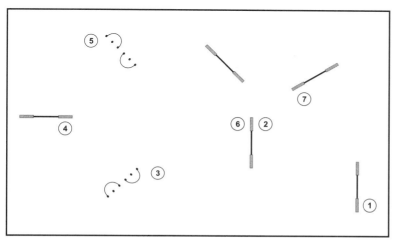

This sequence requires multiple changes of sides, regardless of which side the handler starts the dog on.

Do *not* allow a lead-out. Do one repetition with the dog starting on the handler's left, and one with the dog starting on the handler's right. When starting with the dog on the left, a change of sides will be necessary almost immediately. Then the handler must choose whether to cross prior to the poles or head the dog to jump #4 after the poles. The approach to the second set of poles must be carefully managed to get a clean entry. A rear cross at #6 will probably be required to turn the dog to #7 and avoid the off-course.

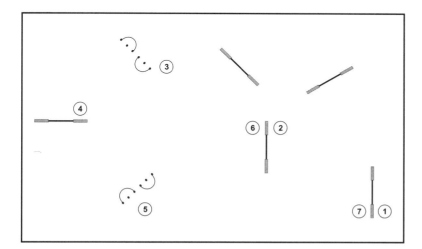

This exercise is deceptively difficult.

Do *not* allow a lead-out. Do one repetition with the dog starting on the handler's left, and one with the dog starting on the handler's right.

If the handler starts with the dog on his left, performance of the first set of poles demands that he decide whether to cross behind the dog for an off-side weave pole performance, or to head the dog out of the poles to jump #4.

The second set of weave poles requires an off-side obtuse entry or a change of sides to get the dog squared up for the entry.

# Set 2

Your set consists of three exercises. The first two exercises use the same equipment set; however, minor equipment movement will be required between exercises.

Your set includes the dogwalk and the A-frame. Remind your students that they should reward their dogs (whether it's with food or with praise) *only* in the contact zone of the descent ramp. The dog is not permitted to leave the contact zone without a quiet release from his handler. If the dog bails off early, he should be picked up and placed back in the contact zone.

Balance your time with each group so that your students get approximately the same amount of work on each of the exercises.

## Run Around Sue

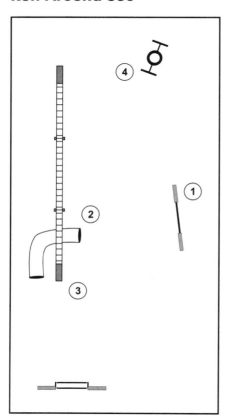

This exercise features a tight turnaround after the pipe tunnel onto the dogwalk at #3. The spread jump might entice some dogs. But mostly a turnaround like this calls for quick handler reaction to get the dog turned early.

Watch to see how your students close the exercise with the turn from the dogwalk to the tire. The handler should work for the down contact zone and not anticipate the turn until the dog is clearly in the yellow.

## Run Around Sue Variation

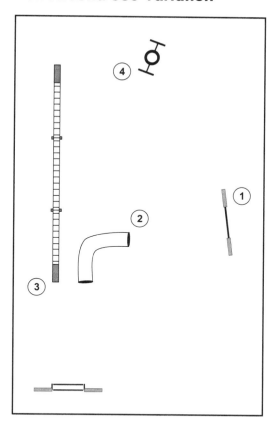

In this exercise, the tunnel is *not* tucked under the dogwalk. Should this cause the handler to worry even more about negotiating a successful turnaround from the pipe tunnel to the dogwalk?

How does this change of configuration effect the handling challenge and the speed of the turnaround?

Which sequence causes your students more difficulty?

## Off-Side Sweep

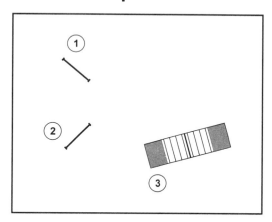

The purpose of this exercise is the execute an off-side sweep to the A-frame. This is more difficult than a heel-side sweep. Many handlers will have no idea that their dogs might have a problem with this maneuver until they encounter it in competition where they will earn an unexpected refusal.

In the transition from jump #2 to the A-frame, the handler should use a *Come!* command to turn the dog neatly to the A-frame. It is also the handler's responsibility to ensure that the dog is squarely lined up for ascending the A-frame.

If you have time, reverse the direction of the set. Continue to work for the down-side contact zone. The dog should not leave the yellow until quietly released by the handler.

# Set 3

Your set consists of two exercises. Major equipment movement will be required between exercises. Brief your students immediately that they will be moving the equipment between exercises. You will lay the jump bars on the ground to indicate where to position jumps. Instruct your students to move the jump standards into place.

Your set includes the see-saw. Remind your students that they should reward their dogs (whether it's with food or with praise) *only* in the contact zone of the descent ramp. The dog is not permitted to leave the contact zone without a quiet release from his handler. If the dog bails off early, he should be picked up and placed back in the contact zone.

You will be responsible for running the fifth part of the eight-week "Raising Jump Heights" program. Be sure to make careful notes of your students' progress so that whoever runs this exercise next week will be properly prepared and can make necessary adjustments.

Balance your time with each group so that your students get approximately the same amount of work on each of the exercises.

## In Front

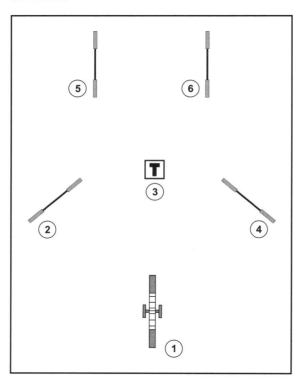

This exercise is designed to "pre-position" the handler in front of his dog so that he can practice various movements while working in front of the dog.

**Call over the see-saw**—Do one repetition with the handler calling the dog over the see-saw. The handler should lead out, taking a position about 6' beyond the see-saw, and then call the dog. Take note of which dogs are *not* slowing to tip the board. You may need a spotter for this exercise.

**NOTE:** The see-saw can be replaced by a jump if calling the dog over the obstacle proves to be too advanced for your students. However, even if the handler starts with his dog, he can use the see-saw to get a position ahead of the dog.

**See-saw to table**—The handler should leave the dog on a stay facing the see-saw and then lead out to a position behind the table. The handler then calls the dog over the see-saw to the table. Do one repetition.

**The scoop**—This repetition begins with the see-saw and the handler leading out as in the previous repetition. However, as soon as the dog clears the down contact of the see-saw, the handler will side step to direct the dog to jump #2.

The handler finishes by rotating back towards the table after the dog commits to jump #2.

Do one repetition each of #1-#2-#3 and #1-#4-#3.

Advanced Agility Workbook

**Slide and scoop**—Have the handler begin this repetition with the see-saw and jump just as he did in the previous repetition, but this time add another jump before going to the table.

The handler should continue to take advantage of being in front of the dog. As the dog commits toward jump #2, the handler will slide up behind jump #5, calling the dog. As the dog commits to jump #5, the handler "scoops" the dog back down to the table.

Do one repetition each of #1-#2-#5-#3 and #1-#4-#6-#3.

**Continuing**—As time permits, do repetitions of the following sequences: #1-#2-#5-#6-#3 and #1-#4-#6-#5-#3; and then #1-#2-#5-#6-#3 and #1-#4-#6-#5-#2-#3.

## Raising Jump Heights

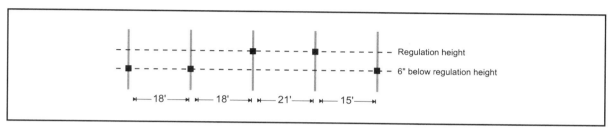

This exercise includes two regulation height jumps in a series of lower jumps. The other jumps in the series are set 6" below the dog's regulation jump height. The jumps are presented to the dog at varied intervals. This spacing is designed to allow the dog to build speed and stride on the approach to the regulation height jumps (the third and fourth jumps).

**NOTE:** For the other exercises this week, the dogs should continue jumping at 6" below their competition height.

Have each dog and handler do at least one repetition of each of the following:

- Leave the dog in a sit-stay behind the first jump, lead out to the third jump, call the dog over the first three jumps, and then complete the sequence running with the dog on the heel-side.

- Leave the dog in a sit-stay behind the first jump, lead out to the third jump, call the dog over the first three jumps, and then complete the sequence running with the dog on the off-side.

- Leave the dog in a sit-stay behind the first jump, lead out past the last jump, and call the dog over all of the entire line of jumps.

**IF A DOG REFUSES THE REGULATION HEIGHT JUMPS:** Back up to Week 3 of the program.

## End Game

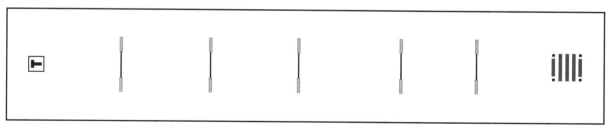

Add the table at the beginning of the line of jumps at least 15' away from the first jump. Add the long jump at the end of the sequence at least 15' away from the first jump. Starting with the dog on the table, have each dog and handler do at least one repetition of each of the previous steps. Set the table and long jump at regulation height.

# Week 5: Student Notes

When an exercise is being performed correctly, you will note that your dog's path and your path form lines that are parallel to each other. This is true regardless of the distance at which your dog works from you.

Every dog has a "comfort zone" for working with his handler. If the handler is working too far away, the dog will come in towards the handler; or, if the handler steps in too close, the dog will move away from the handler. This defines the comfort zone. This zone is quite different for different dogs. For example, a dog may have a narrow comfort zone, far away from his handler. That is, the dog will work at an impressive distance, but will push away from the handler at the slightest body movement that encroaches on the dog's zone.

*Artist: Nancy Krouse-Culley*

The handler's challenge is to establish and then maintain a parallel path to his dog at a distance that is entirely compatible with the dog's comfort zone. So you will see handlers with dogs that work at extreme distances turning very early, setting up a parallel path with quite a bit of distance; while most of us, with dogs who work at a less spectacular distance, can turn and establish a parallel path quite close to our dogs.

Many novice handlers have no idea of striking a parallel path when working in agility, or of their dog's comfort zone. As you practice in class and at home, make note of how your dog turns in relationship to you. It can be very helpful to have someone videotape a training session so that you can study the tape later.

## The Attention Game

The goal of this game is to tune the dog's attention to you. You are teaching the dog to *Watch Me!*. The game was originally designed for the obedience team. But the principles lend themselves quite well to the agility game.

It works like this. Go free heeling with the dog. You might use a leash for obedience, but for agility do *not* use a leash. Introduce a random series of abrupt changes of direction as you heel, or even run, with the dog. As the dog turns and hurries to catch up with you, pop a treat into his mouth. That will make him especially interested in catching up with you. These sudden changes of direction must be as unpredictable (for the dog) as possible.

At first you will find that you are leaving the dog behind at will. As the dog discovers that you've launched yourself in a new direction, he'll hurry to catch up with you, especially now that he knows that he'll be rewarded. As you continue to suddenly and unexpectedly change directions, your dog will begin to get the rules of the game. He will calculate what he needs to do to win the game. He will watch you intently and will leap to head you off at the first sign that you are going to change direction on him again.

You will find that your dog is so keen to win the game that you will begin to have a great deal of difficulty surprising him with changes of direction. Many dogs get so good at the game that they will head you off before you take a complete step in the new direction. You will have to keep a handful of food treats because you are giving them out so frequently.

Once you have taught your dog this game, it becomes a terrific tune-up game prior to going into the ring at competition. This warm-up game will remind your dog to look to you for direction in the course sequence because you can be, after all, quite unpredictable.

# Preparing for Distance Work

The following are some basic skills exercises developed by Nancy Gyes of Foothill Dog Training and Power Paws Agility in San Jose, California. These exercises are useful for continuing to work on distance skills as well as working on control.

Put the dog on a sit-stay in front of a series of jumps as shown in the illustration below. Run away from the dog down the line of jumps. If the dog breaks the sit stay, take him back, place him in a sit without comment, and then praise and *release*. Do not allow the dog to do the series of jumps.

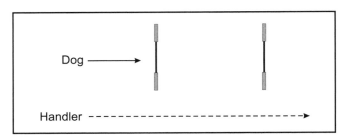

Start the exercise again. If you have to place the dog back in a sit, don't do the series of jumps. Take the dog back, place him in a sit, and then praise and release. Start the exercise again.

Once the dog has stayed quietly and calmly at the start line, call him over the jumps.

Leave the dog in a sit-stay and go to the other side of the table as illustrated. Call the dog over the two jumps to the table. Gradually increase the distance between you and the table. Give the dog a quick *Down!* signal and command as he hits the table. Move closer to the table if the dog slides off; farther away as proficiency is gained.

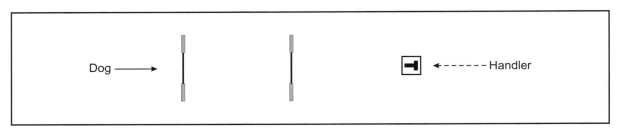

Run with the dog down a line of jumps to the table as illustrated here. You should run *past* the table. The dog is expected to stop and down on the table without you having to slow your forward momentum. Go back to the dog, exaggerate praise *while* the dog is on the table, and give a quiet release.

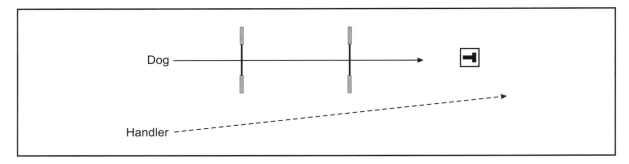

Stand behind the pipe tunnel and call the dog over the jumps and into the tunnel as shown in this illustration.

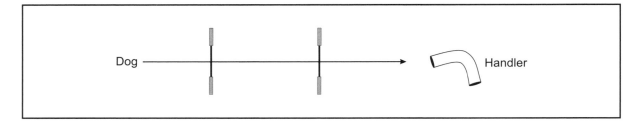

# Week 6: Instructor Notes

From time to time, a dog that has shown great promise will for whatever reason take a step backward in confidence and performance. This can happen for a variety of reasons. The dog may have hurt himself falling off the dogwalk, or startled himself on a see-saw that crashed too hard to the ground. Even an unfamiliar obstacle, like a dogwalk that is bouncy and sways high in the air, can erode a dog's confidence.

*Artist: Valerie Pietraszewska*

You have to be ready to counsel the handler about homework. If it's at all feasible, it's a good idea to keep around a collection of loaner equipment that you can check out to your students in need. You should also have a repertoire of backyard exercises for them.

A dog who is not confident with the bounciness of a high dog may begin to refuse dogwalks altogether. This kind of performance should be solved by backyard training. Be especially careful that the handler doesn't begin to force the dog to the performance. The handler may believe that the dog is being obstinate and willful. If the remedy isn't handled carefully, the long range damage to the dog's training could be significant.

Rather than trying to force or cajole the dog, devise an at home program for the handler to acclimate the dog to the possibility that planks might be bouncy. Tell the handler to go home and place a 12' plank over four cinder blocks. The support of the four blocks will allow no bounce whatsoever. Go out every day for a week and work the dog back and forth. Keep the exercises happy, upbeat, and short. Now, take one of the cinder blocks out, suspending the plank over only three blocks. Again, work the dog every day for a week, back and forth over the plank. Finally, take the center block out, suspending the plank between the two blocks. The plank will be considerably bouncier than before. Work for another week on the bouncy plank. The dog will learn to work even a bouncy plank happily.

Typically a dog will trust his handler until the handler gives the dog reason to think that he might not be trustworthy. As the instructor, you need to always keep your exercises safe and doable. Before each class session, you also need to inspect equipment to ensure that there is nothing in the operation of the equipment that will hurt the dog and damage his faith in you.

| | Set 1 | Set 2 | Set 3 |
|---|---|---|---|
| **Week 6** | **Tunnel Turmoil 1 & 2**<br>*Obstacles:* nonwinged jump, see-saw, two pipe tunnels, double spread hurdle, triple spread hurdle, weave poles | **180° Whoops**<br>*Obstacles:* four winged jumps, tire<br>**Raising Jump Heights**<br>*Obstacles:* four winged jumps, tire<br>*Note:* Major equipment movement is required between exercises. | **Walk Into Pinwheel Peril**<br>*Obstacles:* three winged jumps, dogwalk, A-frame<br>**Blind Ascent**<br>*Obstacles:* A-frame, two winged jumps<br>*Note:* Major equipment movement is required between exercises. |

## Organizational Notes

Review the notes from the Week 5 Progress Worksheets with all of your instructors. Devise a plan for grouping problem students together so that exercises can be simplified and remedial training steps can be taken without disturbing the work of more advanced dogs and handlers.

Make set assignments for your instructors. Try to mix up what sets your instructors are leading so that the instructors get some variety out of teaching.

Begin your training session by doing the control exercise on page 81 with all students. Then break into groups for the training sets if you're going to work multiple sets simultaneously.

# *Week 6: Progress Worksheet*

**Instructors:**                                          **Date:**

| Handler and Dog | Present | Notes |
|---|---|---|
|  |  |  |
|  |  |  |
|  |  |  |
|  |  |  |
|  |  |  |
|  |  |  |
|  |  |  |
|  |  |  |
|  |  |  |
|  |  |  |
|  |  |  |
|  |  |  |

GENERAL NOTES:

# Week 6: Facility Layout

One square = 10'

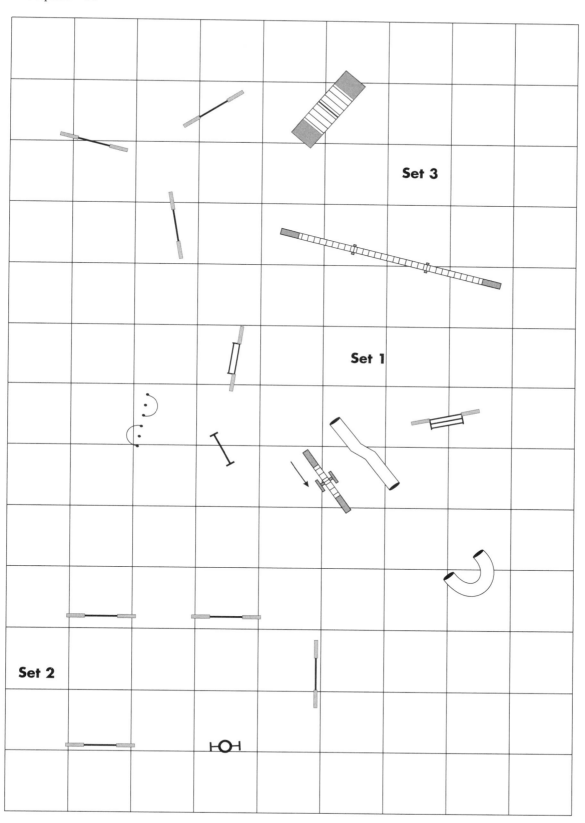

# Week 6: Facility Layout Worksheet

Design your Facility Layout using a 1" = 10' scale (standard agility template)

WEEK 6

# Week 6: Exercises

Start the class by doing the control exercise with everyone. Then break into smaller groups if you're going to work with the training sets simultaneously.

## Control Exercise

- With all of the dogs on-lead, have your students free heel the dogs in a "follow-the-leader" fashion through the field of equipment. Allow the dogs to sniff and inspect the equipment. Take your time. Let the dogs get any desire to sniff and explore out of their systems.

- Organize your students into two lines, facing one another, about 30' apart.

- Next, have a dog and handler across from each other in either line heel their dogs towards one another so that the handlers meet in the middle (with the dogs on their outside). Instruct the handlers to sit their dogs and extend their right hands for a firm handshake. Then instruct the handlers to down their dogs and remain in the center. Have the next pair of handlers and dogs in line perform the same exercise. By the time all of the dogs and handlers have advanced to the middle and completed their handshake, everyone will be in one long line in the middle with the dogs facing alternately in both directions

- Now instruct your students to walk up and down the line of downed dogs, weaving in and out of them, shaking hands with every other student they meet. If any dog breaks his down, that dog's handler should return to the dog, put the dog back in a down position, and then continue weaving through the line of dogs. Don't spend an excessive amount of time doing this.

- Instruct everyone to return to their dogs.

End of exercise.

## Set 1

Your set consists of two exercises that use the same equipment. No equipment movement is required.

Your set includes the see-saw. Remind your students that they should reward their dogs (whether it's with food or with praise) *only* in the contact zone of the descent ramp. The dog is not permitted to leave the contact zone without a quiet release from his handler. If the dog bails off early, he should be picked up and placed back in the contact zone.

Balance your time with each group so that your students get approximately the same amount of work on each of the exercises.

*Artist: Jaci Cotton*

## Tunnel Turmoil 1 & 2

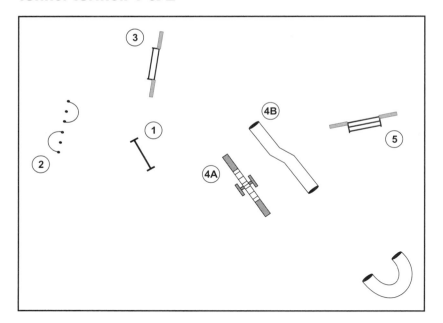

The purpose of this exercise is to get your students working at top speed while negotiating options in the sequence.

Start by using the see-saw as the #4 obstacle after the double spread at #3. The handler will really have to hang back and give a strong *Come!* command to get the dog to turn all the way back to the see-saw. Do this several times and then use the pipe tunnel as the #4 obstacle. How does this change the handler's strategy?

If you have time, try using the curved pipe tunnel as the #5 obstacle instead of the triple spread. Alternate which side of the tunnel you use at #5.

It is rare to see tunnel-tunnel combinations like this in competition, but it makes for an interesting exercise.

Note that the wrong entry to the second tunnel at #3 is framed for the dog as he exits the first tunnel at #2. The handler should change sides to the dog while the dog is in the first tunnel, in order to pull the dog left for the correct entry to the second tunnel.

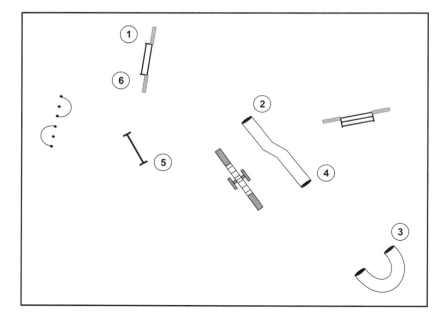

# Set 2

Your set consists of two exercises. Major equipment movement will be required between exercises. Brief your students immediately that they will be moving the equipment between exercises. You will lay the jump bars on the ground to indicate where to position jumps. Instruct your students to move the jump standards into place.

You will be responsible for running the sixth part of the eight-week "Raising Jump Heights" program. Be sure to make careful notes of your students' progress so that whoever runs this exercise next week will be properly prepared and can make necessary adjustments.

Balance your time with each group so that your students get approximately the same amount of work on each of the exercises.

## The 180° Whoops

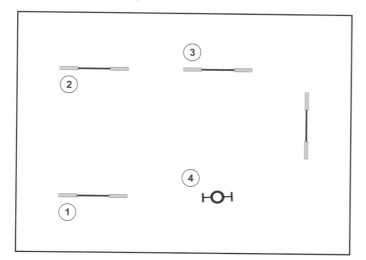

This is a learning experience for the unforeseen off-course.

Tell your students that they are *not* allowed to lead out. For the first repetition, ask them to start with the dog on their right side.

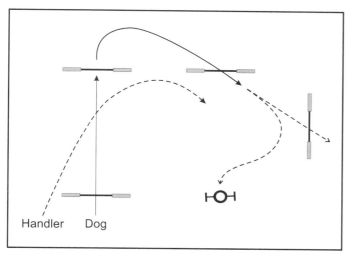

Handler    Dog

Starting with the dog on his right, the handler is likely to try commiting his dog to jump #2, crossing behind the dog, and then turning and calling the dog over jump #3.

The likely result is that the handler will lose his dog to the off-course jump or on a wide, time-consuming path as the dog is tempted by the off-course jump. What went wrong?

What happens if you have the handler start with the dog on his left?

In all likelihood, the results will not be a lot different. Dogs will still veer wide towards the off-course jump.

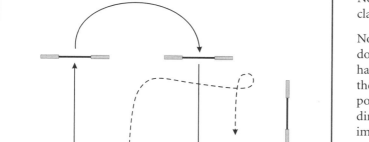

Dog    Handler

Now have handlers try the sequence using a classic counter-rotation manuever as shown.

Note that the handler crosses in front of his dog and then turns *towards* his dog. The handler's objective is to get to the far side of the second jump in the 180° turn. This position allows the handler 1) to call his dog directly over the jump; and 2) dramatically impact the dog's change of direction, pushing him to the correct obstacle at #4.

This maneuver will work even if the handler starts the sequence with the dog on his right. In this case, he would cross behind the dog at jump #2 and then take up a position on the far side of jump #3.

## Raising Jump Heights

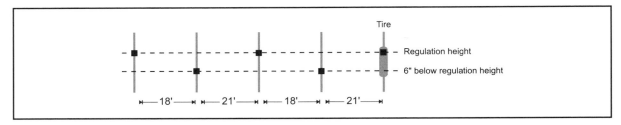

This exercise includes two regulation height jumps *and* a regulation height tire in a series of lower jumps. The other jumps in the series are set 6" below the dog's regulation jump height. The jumps are presented to the dog at varied intervals. This spacing is designed to allow the dog to build speed and stride on the approach to the regulation height jumps (the first and third jumps, and the tire).

**NOTE:** For the other exercises this week, you may want to set a couple of the jumps at regulation height depending on how the class is doing with the "Raising Jump Heights" program.

Have each dog and handler do at least one repetition of each of the following:

- Leave the dog in a sit-stay behind the first jump, lead out to the third jump, call the dog over the first three jumps, and then complete the sequence running with the dog on the heel-side.

- Leave the dog in a sit-stay behind the first jump, lead out to the third jump, call the dog over the first three jumps, and then complete the sequence running with the dog on the off-side.

- Leave the dog in a sit-stay behind the first jump, lead out past the last jump, and call the dog over all of the entire line of jumps and through the tire.

**IF A DOG REFUSES THE REGULATION HEIGHT JUMPS:** Back up to Week 5 or an earlier week of the program. If a dog is still having a significant problem at this point, re-evaluate the dog's weight and level of conditioning. Also assess whether or not the handler is doing enough homework. A significant jumping problem cannot be addressed in a group setting. The handler needs to be working with the dog at home, increasing jump heights only an inch or so at a time.

**IF A DOG REFUSES THE REGULATION HEIGHT TIRE:** Lower the tire to 6" below the dog's regulation height. The handler should give the dog a lot of encouragement. You could use something to shield the dog from running between the tire and the aperture. Industrial strength cling wrap works, or you could use some kind of cutout to block the space under and at the sides of the tire.

# Set 3

Your set consists of two exercises. Major equipment movement will be required between exercises. Brief your students immediately that they will be moving the equipment between exercises. You will lay the jump bars on the ground to indicate where to position jumps. Instruct your students to move the jump standards into place.

Your set includes the dogwalk and the A-frame. Remind your students that they should reward their dogs (whether it's with food or with praise) *only* in the contact zone of the descent ramp. The dog is not permitted to leave the contact zone without a quiet release from his handler. If the dog bails off early, he should be picked up and placed back in the contact zone.

Balance your time with each group so that your students get approximately the same amount of work on each of the exercises.

## Walk Into Pinwheel Peril

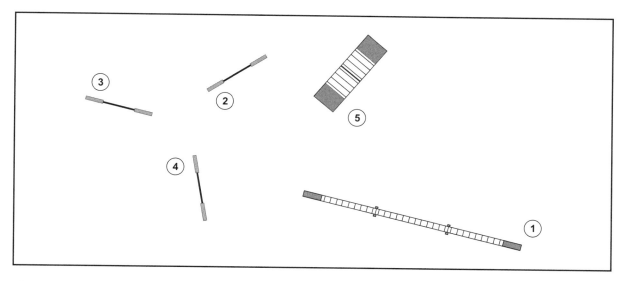

This exercise offers an opportunity for some good contact work for your students and also challenges them to work hard to avoid potential off-courses.

Do *not* allow your students to lead out. Have them do several repetitions starting with the dog on the left side and several starting with the dog on the right side. Does the choice of sides make a difference in how easy or difficult it is to guide the dog from the dogwalk to jump #2?

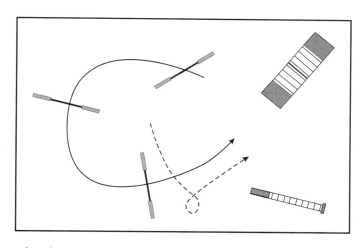

How does the handler deal with the lure of the dogwalk after jump #4 and get the dog turned and squared up for the A-frame?

This might be a good place to have your students work on perfecting their counter-rotation maneuver.

## Blind Ascent

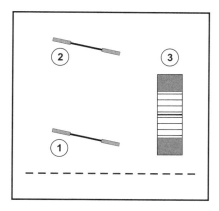

In this exercise, the dog turns 180° off a jump and onto the A-frame. Encourage your students to perform this as in a gamble; that is, the handler must remain behind the line while the dog performs the exercise. If this doesn't work for the dog and handler, they will have to run it together a few times so that the dog can get used to the idea that the handler might not go out with them for this particular exercise.

Usually dog and handler perform the A-frame side-by-side. What impact does the performance coming toward the handler have on the dog's reliability on contacts? Is the dog better? Is the dog worse? Someone should spot the contacts on the ascent side of the A-frame, since the handler may not be able to tell where the dog's feet touch.

Advanced Agility Workbook

# Week 6: Student Notes

Often in agility training, you'll find that the bigger an issue we, the handlers, make out of a training problem, the worse the problem can become for the dog. For example, take the case of a dog that frequently has a problem with the tire. The dog either jumps between the frame and the tire or attempts to duck under the tire. There's a trial coming up and the handler focuses all his efforts on trying to fix the problem before then. However, the next time the dog is in the ring, instead of performing the tire correctly as a result of all this extra training, the dog now completely refuses to even attempt performance of the tire—he runs around the *entire* obstacle. In his attempts to solve a legitimate problem, the handler over-trained on the tire and quickly created a much bigger problem.

*Artist: Rebecca Cheek*

Obviously, you need to address training problems as they occur, and you don't always have the luxury of time. However, here are several things to keep in mind when you tackle a new problem.

- Does the dog fully understand what you are expecting from him? In the tire example, the dog probably doesn't really know what his "job" is with regard to performance of the tire. Therefore, the more you drill on this obstacle, the more frustrated the dog will get and the worse his performance will get until you back up a couple of steps and teach the dog his job.

- Don't start a problem-solving session unless you are armed with plenty of patience. Getting frustrated if the dog progresses slowly (or not at all) is a sure way to stress out both the dog and yourself. If possible, it may be best to take a break from a problem and then come back to it in a few days. You'll give both the dog and yourself a rest and you'll have the opportunity to think of fresh ideas for trying to solve the problem.

- Don't overdrill. Your dog may have a short tolerance for how long he can work on trying to solve a particular problem. Be very creative in how you approach solving the problem and how much training you do. Each dog is different as far as how many repetitions he can take. Some dogs feel that they are not doing the exercise correctly if you repeat it too many times and they will shut down or try a different behavior because they don't think they are pleasing you. Many dogs get bored.

- Do something fun to break up a problem-solving session. For example, set up a fun sequence for your dog using obstacles he really likes or just stop and play with your dog!!

- Break down the problem as much as possible and set interim goals. Design exercises that allow the dog frequent success. The more successes your dog enjoys on the way to solving the big problem, the more it will build both your confidence and his.

## Preparing for Distance Work

At this point in your training, you and your dog have worked lots of exercises (both at home and in class) that focus on honing your dog's response to one of the directional commands: *Come!*, *Get Out!*, or *Go!*.

This week's homework exercises will give you a chance to practice using several of these commands in the *same* exercise. Also make sure that you leave some time in each training session for some weave pole work!

## Putting Directionals Together

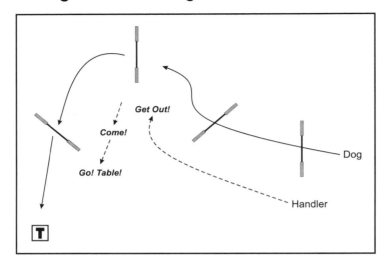

In this exercise, you need to briefly step in towards the dog after jump #2 and give the directional command *Get Out!*. After jump #3, you will need to turn abruptly and call the dog to *Come!*. You should not assume that the dog will turn. Without a well-timed *Come!* command, the dog might run out past the fourth jump.

After jump #4, tell the dog to *Go! Table!*. Bait the table to help entice the dog. With each repetition, start to hang back at jump #4, trusting the dog to go on.

Do this exercise at least once a day for two or three days.

## *Come!* and the Option

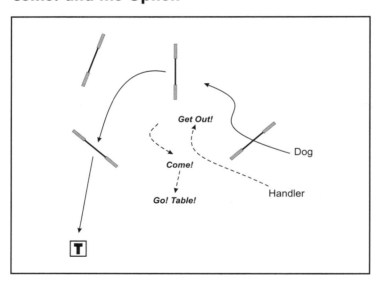

An "option" is a place in a course where the sequence can go one way or another. In this case, the dog sees the jump ahead and might assume that it's the next correct obstacle, unless the handler skillfully intervenes.

As before, you will rely on a *Come!* command to turn the dog. But in this case, you will also add body movement, back-pedaling away from the off-course jump. This exaggerated movement to influence the dog's course is called "hanging back".

Do this exercise at least once a day for two or three days.

## *Go!* and the Option

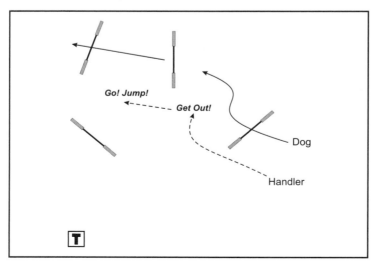

In this exercise, the dog's option is to go on to the next obvious jump, or to turn left for the jump-tunnel combination.

You will take an extra step or two after jump #2 and command your dog to Go! and to *Jump!* Again your command is key, but movement is helpful as well.

Do this exercise at least once a day for two or three days.

WEEK 6

# Week 7: Instructor Notes

Do you have dogs in class that aren't entirely fit to compete? It's not unusual to have dogs that are out of condition or overweight, especially if your class attracts a lot of pet dogs. Many pet owners don't have the knowledge or the will to give their dogs a proper fitness program.

What do you do with the dog that weighs about twice what he should weigh? The dog might be very good natured and does everything asked of him, but is not physically capable of the obstacle performance he is asked to do. How do you tactfully put it to the handler that the dog should be on a fitness program?

One approach is to have a fitness litmus test so that you can demonstrate to the dog's owner that a diet would be in order.

*Artist: Rebecca Cheek*

Can you feel all of the dog's ribs under your fingers without applying pressure? Run your hand over the dog's rump. There is a bone over each hip that you should be able to feel without probing around. If the dog passed both of these tests he is probably at a good weight. If you didn't feel the ribs or the bones, then the dog needs exercise and diet.

The hard part about a diet is that the dog wants to eat and he will follow the handler around the house with his big, sad, begging, puppy-dog eyes. It's hard not to feed the pup when he feels the hollow in his stomach. The answer is to supplement the dog's regular feeding with fillers that are healthy and filling. Advise the handler of the overweight dog to cut back on the dog's regular rations and supplement it with boiled rice and green beans. If you can cultivate an appetite for green things you can give the dog almost as much as he wants to eat without having him on a fattening diet. Follow a calorie counter to decide which greens might be better than others. Avoid canned greens that are loaded with sodium.

| | Set 1 | Set 2 | Set 3 |
|---|---|---|---|
| **Week 7** | **Utility Agility**<br>*Obstacles:* four winged jumps<br><br>**Raising Jump Heights**<br>*Obstacles:* four winged jumps, tire, long jump, table<br><br>*Note:* Major equipment movement is required between exercises. | **Go Tunnel!**<br>*Obstacles:* dogwalk, two winged jumps, double spread hurdle, collapsed tunnel, two pipe tunnels | **Murphy Shoulda Said It**<br>*Obstacles:* three winged jumps, two nonwinged jumps, A-frame<br><br>**Depressed Bootlace**<br>*Obstacles:* A-frame, five winged jumps<br><br>*Note:* Major equipment movement is required between exercises. |

## Organizational Notes

Review the notes from the Week 6 Progress Worksheets with all of your instructors. Devise a plan for grouping problem students together so that exercises can be simplified and remedial training steps can be taken without disturbing the work of more advanced dogs and handlers. Once again, if you have time prior to class, put a dog through each of the sets so that the instructors will understand the exercises for the day.

When you make your set assignments this week, remind the instructor who is responsible for the "Raising Jump Heights" exercise that *three* substitution obstacles will be used today: 1) table; 2) long jump; and 3) tire. Therefore, the exercise will be somewhat labor intensive.

Begin your training session by doing the control exercise on page 93 with all students. Then break into groups for the training sets if you're going to work multiple sets simultaneously.

# Week 7: Progress Worksheet

**Instructors:**                                           **Date:**

| Handler and Dog | Present | Notes |
|---|---|---|
|  |  |  |
|  |  |  |
|  |  |  |
|  |  |  |
|  |  |  |
|  |  |  |
|  |  |  |
|  |  |  |
|  |  |  |
|  |  |  |
|  |  |  |
|  |  |  |

GENERAL NOTES:

# Week 7: Facility Layout

One square = 10'

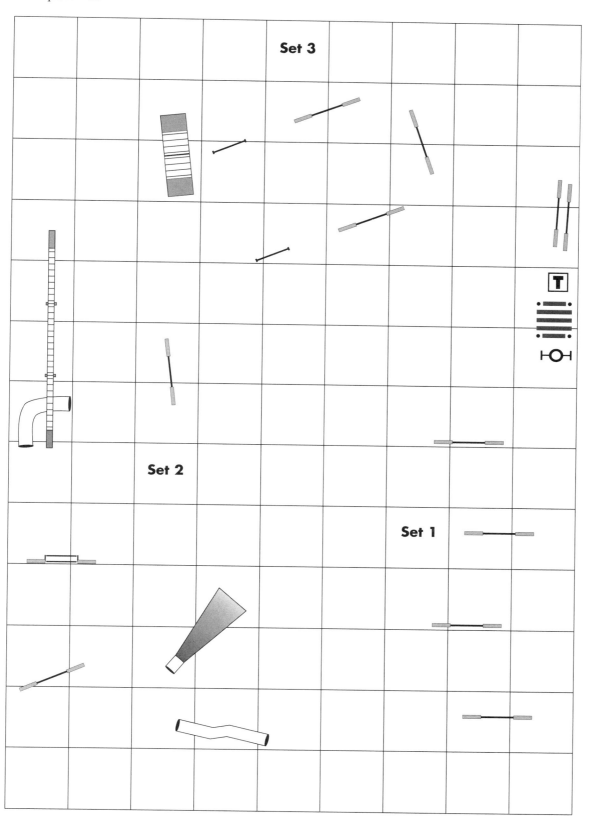

Set 3

Set 2

Set 1

WEEK 7

# Week 7: Facility Layout Worksheet

Design your Facility Layout using a 1" = 10' scale (standard agility template)

# Week 7: Exercises

Start the class by doing the control exercise with everyone. Then break into smaller groups if you're going to work the training sets simultaneously.

## Control Exercise

- With all of the dogs on-lead, have your students free heel the dogs in a "follow-the-leader" fashion through the field of equipment. Allow the dogs to sniff and inspect the equipment. Take your time. Let the dogs get any desire to sniff and explore out of their systems.

- Instruct your students that you will now do an attention exercise. The purpose of the exercise is to work on the *Come!* command with a bit of motivation added using the leash. Have everyone free heel their dogs on-lead simultaneously, but individually rather than in a follow-the-leader queue. About every ten seconds each handler should unexpectedly change direction, giving the dog a *Come!* command. If the dog doesn't immediately change direction to match the handler's new direction, the handler should give a crisp "pop" on the leash to remind the dog that the *Come!* is not optional. Tell your students that the ideal moment to change direction and command the dog to *Come!* is when the dog is approaching an obstacle or another dog.

End of exercise.

## Set 1

Your set consists of two exercises. Major equipment movement will be required between exercises. Brief your students immediately that they will be moving the equipment between exercises. You will lay the jump bars on the ground to indicate where to position jumps. Instruct your students to move the jump standards into place.

You will be responsible for running the seventh part of the eight-week "Raising Jump Heights" program. Be sure to make careful notes about any students that are still having problems with regulation height jumps.

Balance your time with each group so that your students get approximately the same amount of work on each of the exercises.

### Utility Agility

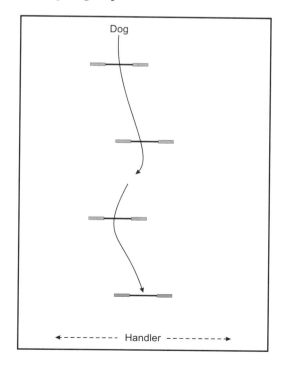

This exercise was developed by Nancy Gyes of Foothill Dog Training and Power Paws Agility in San Jose, California. The ultimate goal is for the dog to start from a central position and for the handler to remain stationary, using hand signals alone to direct the dog over the jumps.

Have the handler leave the dog on a sit-stay behind the first jump. The handler will stand behind an imaginary line as shown in the illustration here and then call the dog over the jumps. The handler can move along this line and use hand signals as necessary to direct the dog over the jumps.

It may be advisable to first attempt this exercise with just two jumps, then three, and then four.

## Raising Jump Heights

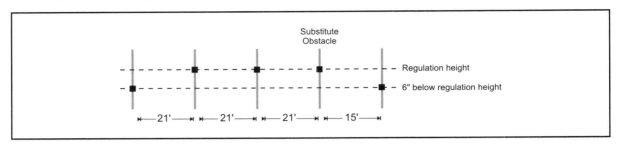

This exercise includes two regulation height jumps *and* a regulation height long jump, or tire (the substitute obstacle in the illustration) in a series of lower jumps. The other jumps in the series are set 6" below the dog's regulation jump height. The jumps are presented to the dog at varied intervals. This spacing is designed to allow the dog to build speed and stride on the approach to the regulation height obstacles (the second, third, and fourth obstacles).

**NOTE:** For the other exercises this week, you may want to set a couple of the jumps at regulation height depending on how the class is doing with the "Raising Jump Heights" program.

Have each dog and handler do at least one repetition of each of the following:

- Leave the dog in a sit-stay behind the first jump, lead out to the third jump, call the dog over the first three jumps, and then complete the sequence running with the dog on the heel-side.

- Leave the dog in a sit-stay behind the first jump, lead out to the third jump, call the dog over the first three jumps, and then complete the sequence running with the dog on the off-side.

- Leave the dog in a sit-stay behind the first jump, lead out past the last jump, and call the dog over all of the entire line of jumps and through the tire.

Change the substitute obstacle and repeat these steps.

**IF A DOG REFUSES THE REGULATION HEIGHT JUMPS:** Back up to Week 5 or an earlier week of the program. If a dog is still having a significant problem at this point, re-evaluate the dog's weight and level of conditioning. Also assess whether or not the handler is doing enough homework. A significant jumping problem cannot be addressed in a group setting. The handler needs to be working with the dog at home, increasing jump heights only an inch or so at a time.

## Set 2

Your set consists of three exercises that use the same equipment set. No equipment movement will be required except reversing the direction of the spread hurdle for the third exercise.

Your set includes the dogwalk. Remind your students that they should reward their dogs (whether it's with food or with praise) *only* in the contact zone of the descent ramp. The dog is not permitted to leave the contact zone without a quiet release from his handler. If the dog bails off early, he should be picked up and placed back in the contact zone.

Balance your time with each group so that your students get approximately the same amount of work on each of the exercises.

# Go Tunnel!

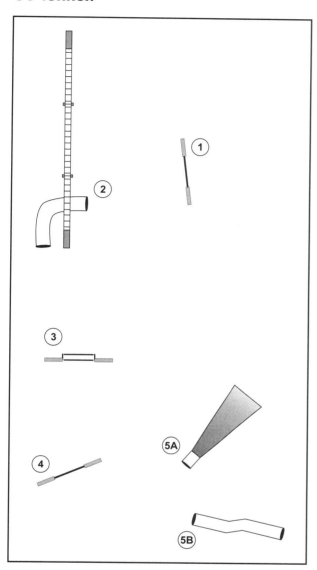

This is a good opportunity to teach your students a very simple rule of dog agility: You give the dog a command for an obstacle *after* you have got him focused on that obstacle.

Alternate which tunnel you have your students perform after jump #4.

Obviously the handler yelling *Tunnel!* after jump #4 is making the exercise dog's choice. Either answer is right to the dog. The handler is going to have to make some body position and timing decisions.

If the turn is to the collapsed tunnel at #5A, the handler will have to hang back, not advancing as far as jump #4, to get the dog looking back. Then it's *Come! Come! Come!*, until the dog is directed back and square to the collapsed tunnel. At that point, the handler should give the *Tunnel!* command.

If the turn is to the pipe tunnel at #5B, the handler can easily step into the pocket and push the dog out. This is a good place for a *Get Out!* command.

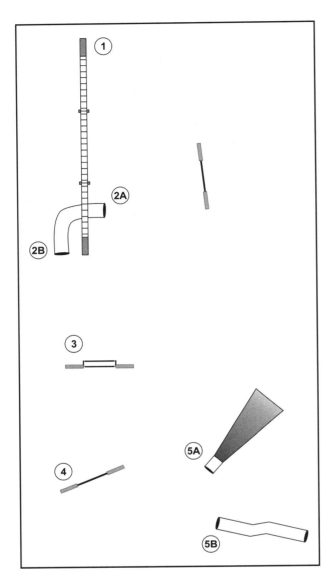

In this renumbered version of the exercise, have your students start the sequence by putting their dogs over the dogwalk. Then with each repetition, alternately have them turn the dog left (#2A) or right (#2B) off the dogwalk into the pipe tunnel. Do the final sequence of obstacles, #3 through #5A or #5B, as you have already been doing them (that is, alternating which tunnel is performed as the closing obstacle).

You have introduced a new challenge in this exercise. When the handler turns the dog left off the dogwalk to the pipe tunnel at #2A, the approach to the double bar spread creates a line that runs *past* jump #4. How many of your students will be ready for this approach? What is the solution?

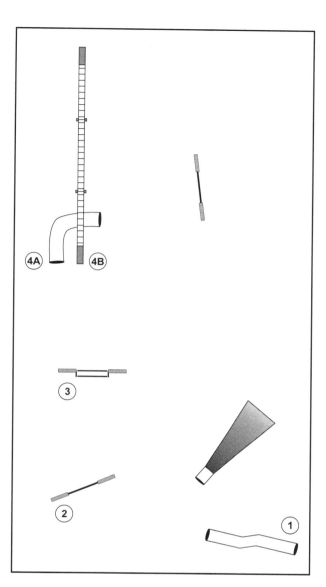

In this renumbered exercise, you will reverse the direction of the flow. To do this, you will have to reverse the direction of the spread hurdle.

With each repetition, alternate which obstacle you have your students perform after the spread hurdle at #3—either the pipe tunnel at #4A or the dogwalk at #4B.

Two significant challenges await the handler. The most obvious is the discrimination problem at the pipe tunnel and dogwalk. In a way, this is similar to the proximity of the two tunnels when the set was heading the other direction. However, the flow is quite fast and the proximity of the two discrimination exercises is less than generous.

A challenge less obvious in this set is the awkward handling line created from the opening sequence to the spread hurdle. The little dogs should negotiate this sequence without much problem. But bigger dogs will be moving very fast and won't have as much room to make adjustments in path.

# Set 3

Your set consists of three exercises. The first two exercises use the same equipment set, however, major equipment movement will be required between the second and third exercises. Brief your students immediately that they will be moving the equipment between exercises. You will lay the jump bars on the ground to indicate where to position jumps. Instruct your students to move the jump standards into place.

Your set includes the A-frame. Remind your students that they should reward their dogs (whether it's with food or with praise) *only* in the contact zone of the descent ramp. The dog is not permitted to leave the contact zone without a quiet release from his handler. If the dog bails off early, he should be picked up and placed back in the contact zone.

Balance your time with each group so that your students get approximately the same amount of work on each of the exercises.

## Murphy Shoulda Said It

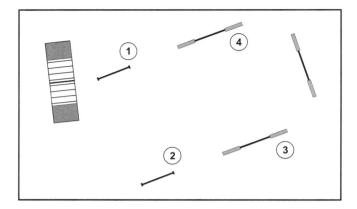

Set up this exercise for your class. Do *not* allow handlers to lead out.

What results do your students get?

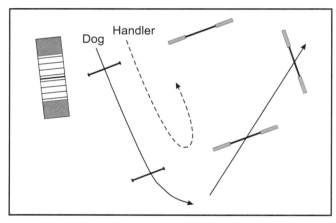

The exercise was designed with the intention that a dog would see the off-course jump as he comes off the turn and take it, when the handler attempts the set with at-side handling as shown in the illustration.

This gives the instructor an opportunity to teach the counter-rotation handling maneuver to help students overcome the problem.

But suppose that no dog takes the off-course. So all of your students scratch their heads and wonder what the heck you are talking about while you try to explain a handling maneuver that nobody apparently needs.

Now you're on the spot to modify the exercise so that it produces the intended result.

What happens if you reverse the set as shown in this illustration?

You should find that the dogs are more than happy to take the off-course over the A-frame after jump #3. Set the A-frame at about 5' so that it's *very* inviting.

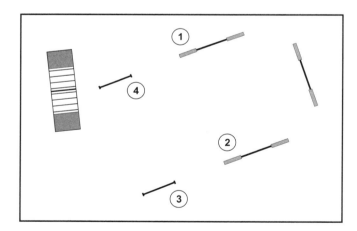

This should allow you to teach a front cross and a counter-rotation maneuver with a clear illustration of the benefit of doing it versus the pitfall of *not* doing it.

WEEK 7

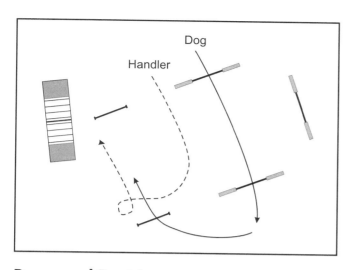

For those of you who need the refresher, a counter-rotation means that the handler rotates back *towards* the dog, *counter* to the flow of the sequence, in order to redirect the dog's path.

The handler in this case is running to his right but pivots back to the left on the far side of #3 after crossing in front of the dog's approach to #3. The maneuver allows the handler to always have the dog in his view and puts the handler between the dog and A-frame, effectively reducing the chance of an off-course.

## Depressed Boot Lace

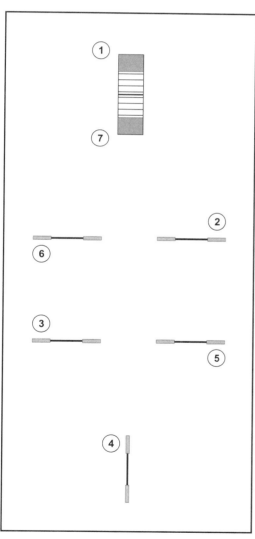

A depressed approach to an obstacle means that the approach is at an acute angle. Often dogs will not recognize that the obstacle is being presented for performance when the approach is depressed. Consider, for instance, that if a jump that is 5' is presented with a 45° turn, then the jump appears to be only 2-1/2' wide in the dog's view.

If a jump is presented with a 90° turn, the jump will have no dimension of width at all. You can't get any more depressed than 90°. It means that the obstacle is presented perpendicular to the dog's path. However, you can expect to see this kind of thing in competition with some regularity.

In this exercise, the A-frame may build initial speed into the series of jumps. The dog's path after jump #2 is away from jump #3. How does the handler deal with the transition? He can either hang back in the pocket and call the dog back in, before pushing out to #3. Or, he could cross in front, counter-rotate and pull the dog around him to jump #3.

Jump #4 is set perpendicular to jumps #3 and #5. However, given the dog's path, if the handler will just get the dog turned, the jump will be presented very nicely.

The transition from #5 to #6 is identical to the #2 to #3 transition. Again, the handler can pull the dog back into him using *Come!* and then kick the dog out over #6; or, he can step into the pocket, counter-rotate and turn the dog around him to jump #6.

The handler should take care to square his dog up adequately for the A-frame at #7.

# Week 7: Student Notes

To compete in agility *and* stay healthy and injury-free, a dog must be in good condition and free of excess pounds. If you have a dog that consistently exhibits a lack of motivation or refuses regulation height obstacles, the root of the problem may very well be physical.

Your job as the dog's owner and handler is to objectively assess your dog's weight and conditioning. Put aside all the books that recommend a range of weight for a particular breed of dog and any preconceived notions that you have about what your dog should look like at his "proper" weight, and perform the following tests.

First do a visual check. Looking down at your dog when he's standing, can you see a clearly defined waist? There should be some gradation between the back of the dog's rib cage and his hips. Looking at the dog from the side, does his abdomen "tuck up" rather than sag down?

*Artist: Nancy Krouse-Culley*

Now do a hands on check. Can you feel all of the dog's ribs under your fingers without applying any pressure? The best way to assess this is to stand next to your dog, facing his tail. Using both hands, place your thumbs side-by-side on top of your dog's backbone and spread your fingers along the dog's rib cage. Move your hands back and forth without pressing. Next, run your hand over the dog's rump. There is a bone over each hip that you should be able to feel without probing around.

If the dog passed all of these tests, he is probably at a good weight. If you didn't feel the ribs or the bones, then the dog needs exercise and diet.

The hard part about a diet is that the dog wants to eat and he will follow you around the house with his big, sad, begging, puppy-dog eyes. It's hard not to feed the pup when he feels the hollow in his stomach. The answer is to supplement the dog's regular feeding with fillers that are healthy and filling. Cut back on the dog's regular rations and supplement it with boiled rice and green beans. If you can cultivate an appetite for green things you can give the dog almost as much as he wants to eat without having him on a fattening diet. Follow a calorie counter to decide which greens might be better than others. Avoid canned greens that are loaded with sodium.

## Reversing Poles and Tunnel Switch

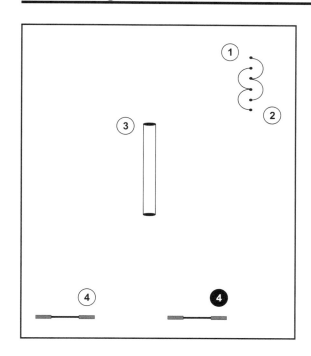

This exercise requires a back-to-back performance of the weave poles and concludes with alternate jumps from the collapsed tunnel.

The exercise requires you to make some choices about which side to work your dog. The double performance of the poles, for instance, offers four distinct possibilities for choice of sides. Try *each* of these handling choices at least twice—once using the white #4 jump to complete the sequence and once using the black #4 jump. It's possible that you will learn something useful about your working relationship with your dog. And, just because the first solution you try works, does not mean that it's necessarily the best solution for your dog.

If you are working with channel wires on your weave poles at home, you should be working towards removing those wires if you haven't already started doing this. Start removing wires from the center of the poles. The last wires you remove are the ones for entry.

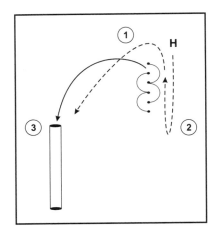

### Right, Then Left

In this choice, you start your dog into the poles on the off-side (your right). At the end of the poles, you turn the dog and, remaining on the same side of the poles, put the dog back through the poles on the heel-side. At the end of the #2 poles, you must turn the dog sharply left for the entry to the tunnel.

This is not as simple as it looks, and you risk a collision with the dog. But the maneuver is certainly do-able. You can either "head" or push the dog sharply to the left, or step behind the dog and pull him (on your right) to the tunnel.

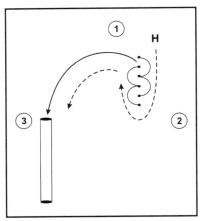

### Right, Then Right

Using this strategy, you must work for an efficient re-entry to the poles. Attempting to off-side heel the dog as shown in the illustration might be the unfortunate choice, since you risk a collision with the dog.

You could turn the dog, push him into the poles at #2, and then step into heel position. However, this maneuver requires considerable practice so that the dog is comfortable with the maneuver and won't pop out of the poles. You might also step behind the dog, counter-rotate and pull the dog into the weave pole entry.

At the conclusion of weave poles at #2, you only have to turn, and pull the dog back into the tunnel.

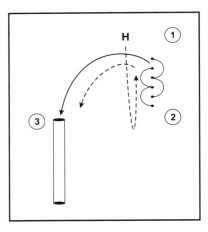

### Left, Then Right

Using this strategy, you start with the dog in the off-side position (your right). At the conclusion of the first performance of the weave poles, you simply turn the dog back to re-enter the poles in the heel position.

At the conclusion of weave poles at #2, you only have to turn and pull the dog back into the tunnel.

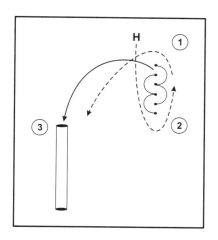

## Left, Then Left

Using this strategy, you start with the dog at heel-side (your left). At the conclusion of the first performance of the weave poles, you are again faced with getting the dog back into the poles while avoiding the possible collision from a heeling type of performance (see the "Right, Then Right" solution).

# Preparing for Distance Work

Here is another exercise to help you work on increasing your dog's ability to work at a distance from you.

## Back-chaining the Send

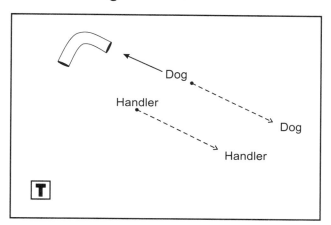

In class, you have worked on sending your dog to the table, over a jump. You can do the same work with a tunnel, or any other obstacle you have available in your backyard.

For the first exercise, send your dog to the pipe tunnel and greet him with a reward and praise when he exits. Start close to the tunnel and then gradually back way a few steps at a time. Before too long you should be able to get some pretty good distance on your send-away to the tunnel.

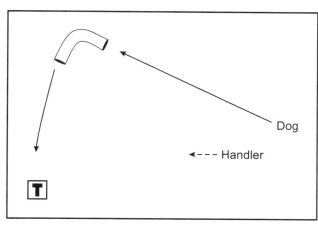

Combine this exercise with the send to table exercise. After sending your dog to the tunnel, step forward towards the table and give him a *Go! Table!* command. You should use bait on the table to reward the performance.

You can alternate sending your dog to the tunnel and calling him back to you, with sending him to the tunnel and then on to the table. This makes your dog keen to listen to you, never knowing what it is you might do next. You just be sure to be very consistent in the way you praise and give your dog treats. And never never use emotional or physical corrections with your dog for failing to do what you wanted or expected him to do. By the way, once you've mastered this particular double send-away, you've learned the most basic novice gamble. You will see this gamble time and time again in agility competition.

# Week 8: Instructor Notes

Being an instructor often means that you make sacrifices in training your own dogs, so that you can give your students the attention they need. It's like the old saying "the cobbler's child goes barefoot." You wind up neglecting important work that you should be doing with your own dog because you don't have enough time, or because you don't have access to the training facility when you're not instructing.

This is the eighth week of a training program and it's probably time that you started thinking of yourself again. How is your own personal agility training program going? Are your dogs getting a good agility workout every week? Are they learning new skills? Are you keeping your dogs in top physical and mental condition?

*Artist: Jo Ann Mather*

The remarkable thing about being an instructor is that you learn a great deal about how dogs work and how they are motivated by observing the ongoing tribulations of your students. You can take this knowledge to your own training program. But there is no substitute for working with your own dog as often as possible so that you can develop and maintain that special working relationship that makes the difference between qualifying and not qualifying. So, make plans to get back to work with your dog. If it means taking a sabbatical from instructing for awhile then you should cut it loose and go back to being a handler for awhile. You won't regret it.

|  | Set 1 | Set 2 | Set 3 |
|---|---|---|---|
| **Week 8** | **Corner 1, 2 and 3** *Obstacles:* A-frame, weave poles, collapsed tunnel, three winged jumps<br><br>**Raising Jump Heights** *Obstacles:* five winged jumps<br><br>*Note:* Major equipment movement is required between exercises. | **Loop de Loops** *Obstacles:* dogwalk, four winged jumps, one nonwinged jump, table (or another nonwinged jump), pipe tunnel | **T Trouble and More T Trouble** *Obstacles:* see-saw, pipe tunnel, tire, table<br><br>**Oopsi! Change of Direction and Revisionist Oopsi!** *Obstacles:* six winged jumps<br><br>*Note:* Major equipment movement is required between exercises. |

## Organizational Notes

This is the last class. As you begin this class, you should compliment your students on their hard work and dedication, and the progress they have made in fine-tuning the working relationship with their dogs.

Attend to any housekeeping related to getting your students re-registered for the next advanced class.

Begin your training session by doing the control exercise on page 109 with all students. Then break into groups for the training sets if you're going to work multiple sets simultaneously.

# *Week 8: Progress Worksheet*

**Instructors:**  Date:

| Handler and Dog | Present | Notes |
|---|---|---|
| | | |
| | | |
| | | |
| | | |
| | | |
| | | |
| | | |
| | | |
| | | |
| | | |
| | | |
| | | |

GENERAL NOTES:

WEEK 8

# Week 8: Facility Layout

One square = 10'

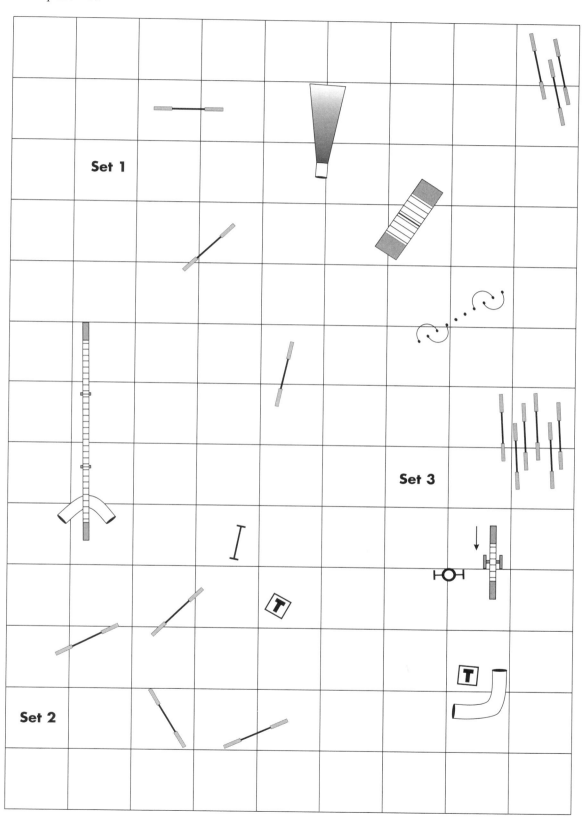

WEEK 8

# Week 8: Facility Layout Worksheet

Design your Facility Layout using a 1" = 10' scale (standard agility template)

# Week 8: Exercises

Start the class by doing the control exercise with everyone. Then break into smaller groups if you're going to work the training sets simultaneously.

## Control Exercise

- With all of the dogs on-lead, have your students free heel the dogs in a "follow-the-leader" fashion through the field of equipment. Allow the dogs to sniff and inspect the equipment. Take your time. Let the dogs get any desire to sniff and explore out of their systems.

- Organize your students into two lines, facing one another, about 30' apart.

- Next, have a dog and handler across from each other in either line heel their dogs towards one another so that the handlers meet in the middle (with the dogs on their outside). Instruct the handlers to sit their dogs and extend their right hands for a firm handshake. Then instruct the handlers to down their dogs and remain in the center. Have the next pair of handlers and dogs in line perform the same exercise. By the time all of the dogs and handlers have advanced to the middle and completed their handshake, everyone will be in one long line in the middle with the dogs facing alternately in both directions

- Now instruct your students to walk up and down the line of downed dogs, weaving in and out of them, shaking hands with every other student they meet. If any dog breaks his down, that dog's handler should return to the dog, put the dog back in a down position, and then continue weaving through the line of dogs. Don't spend an excessive amount of time doing this.

- Instruct everyone to return to their dogs.

End of exercise.

## Set 1

Your set consists of four exercises. The first three exercises use the same equipment. However, major equipment movement is required between the third and fourth exercises. Brief your students immediately that they will be moving the equipment between exercises. You will lay the jump bars on the ground to indicate where to position jumps. Instruct your students to move the jump standards into place.

You will be responsible for running the last part of the "Raising Jump Heights" program. Have a homework program ready for any students that are still having problems with regulation height jumps. In addition, you also need to be ready with a recommendation for each student as to whether his dog is ready to do regulation-height jumping in the next advanced class or whether he needs to repeat the "Raising Jump Heights" program.

Balance your time with each group so that your students get approximately the same amount of work on each of the exercises.

*Artist: Jaci Cotton*

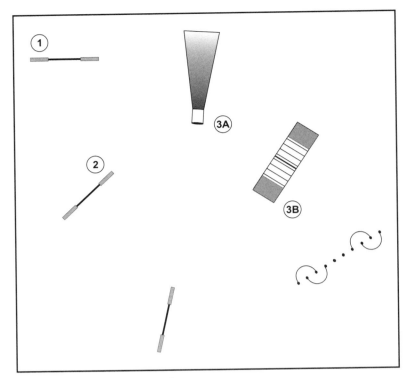

## Corner 1, 2 and 3

This first exercise pitches the dog into a call-off situation, with the off-course jump after jump #2, and then turns the dog to an alternating finish at #3.

Have your students do at least one repetition using each of the two alternative finishing obstacles.

Also have your students alternate the start. Try the exercise starting with the dog on the right, the dog on the left, and a handler lead-out.

When turning to the A-frame at #3B after jump #2, the handler will need to pull his dog in (away from the off-course jump), and then push out, to give the dog sufficient room to square up for the ascent.

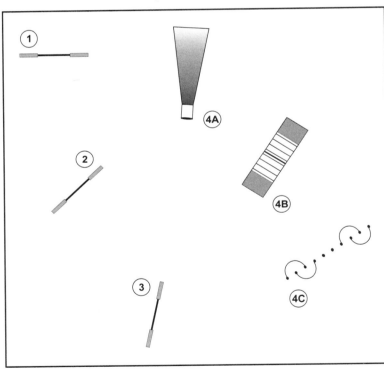

In this renumbered sequence, there are *three* obstacles to use as the last obstacle in the sequence.

Have your students do at least one repetition using each of the three alternatives.

Remember, this is *not* a handler's choice exercise. Be sure to specify which closing obstacle you want the students to use for each repetition.

Each of the three closing obstacles—collapsed tunnel, A-frame, or weave poles—are taken off a left turn. Only the degree of the turn is different for each.

Remind your students that the first job is to get the dog pointed in the direction of the correct obstacle. Only then should a command for the obstacle be given.

Intermediate Agility Workbook

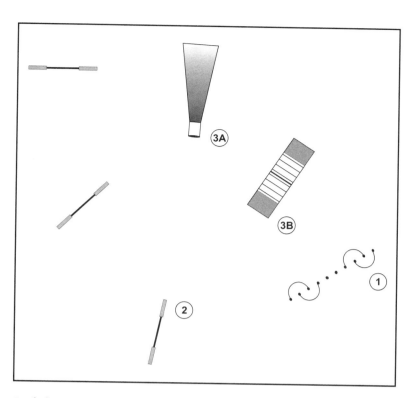

This companion exercise again pitches the dog into a call-off situation, with the off-course jump after jump #2, and turns the dog to an alternating finish at #3.

Have your students do at least one repetition using each of the two alternative finishing obstacles.

Also have your students alternate the start. Try the exercise starting with the dog on the right, the dog on the left, and a handler lead-out.

How is the turn after jump #2 to each of the finishing obstacles influenced by each of the possible starting positions?

## Raising Jump Heights

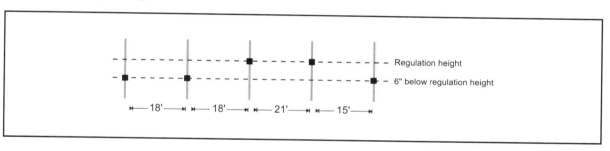

This is the final week of an eight-week program to raise the dog's jump height to regulation height. At the end of this class, you should make a recommendation to the handler for the next advanced class to either begin working with a group that is working at full height, or to take the jump height program yet again and work with a group that is working at a lower jump height. Use the notes that you've been taking over the course of the program to make your determination.

This exercise includes two regulation height jumps in a series of lower jumps. The other jumps in the series are set 6" below the dog's regulation jump height. The jumps are presented to the dog at varied intervals. This spacing is designed to allow the dog to build speed and stride on the approach to the regulation height obstacles (the third, and fourth jumps).

Have each dog and handler do at least one repetition of each of the following:

- Leave the dog in a sit-stay behind the first jump, lead out to the third jump, call the dog over the first three jumps, and then complete the sequence running with the dog on the heel-side.

- Leave the dog in a sit-stay behind the first jump, lead out to the third jump, call the dog over the first three jumps, and then complete the sequence running with the dog on the off-side.

WEEK 8

Raise the height of the second jump to regulation height, and have each dog and handler repeat the two steps.

Next, raise the height of the fifth jump, and have each dog and handler repeat the two steps.

Finally, raise the height of the first jump, and have each dog and handler repeat the two steps.

**IF A DOG REFUSES THE REGULATION HEIGHT JUMPS:** You should recommend that the handler repeat the jump height program with his dog in the next advanced program.

# Set 2

Your set consists of five exercises that use the same equipment set. No equipment movement will be required.

Your set includes the dogwalk. Remind your students that they should reward their dogs (whether it's with food or with praise) *only* in the contact zone of the descent ramp. The dog is not permitted to leave the contact zone without a quiet release from his handler. If the dog bails off early, he should be picked up and placed back in the contact zone.

Balance your time with each group so that your students get approximately the same amount of work on each of the exercises.

## Loop de Loops

This group of exercises was designed by Linda Mecklenburg of Ostrander, Ohio. They are based on a segment of a USDAA Masters titling class designed by Bill Sterling of Columbus, OH. The exercises are designed so that once the obstacles are set, they may be renumbered without moving them. Each exercise presents a different handler challenge. There is no right or wrong way to perform any of these exercises. Hopefully, your students will be creative and determine for themselves (with your expert tips, of course) what is successful.

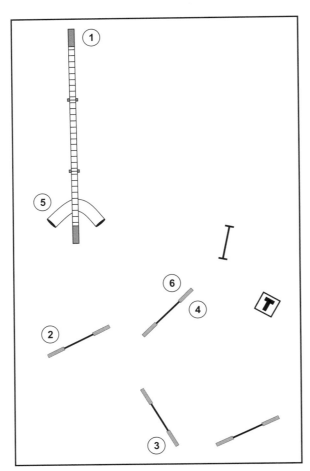

This is the kind of sequence in which a solid dogwalk performance will come in handy. The tunnel represents a minor handler restriction. The handler needs to position his body to direct the dog away from the straight-ahead jump, and to jump #2 instead.

The transition from #4 to #5 to #6 will be most interesting. How do your students manage the sequence to avoid the multiple opportunities for the dog to go off-course?

Intermediate Agility Workbook

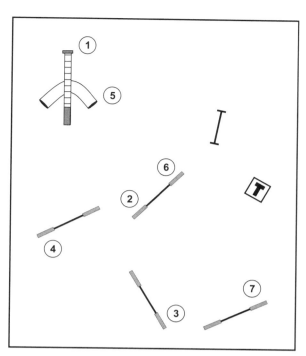

This sequence will be relatively fast. The main challenge is getting the dog to cross from #4 to the pipe tunnel at #5 while avoiding the off-course end of the pipe tunnel, and the dogwalk.

Ideally, the handler will figure out how to get ahead of the dog to manage the sequence.

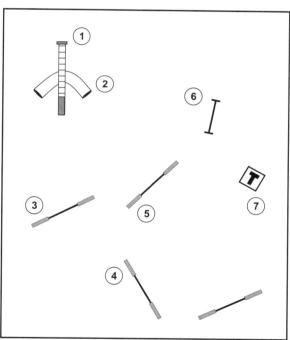

In this sequence, the handler is faced with stuffing the dog into the pipe tunnel, which is tucked under the descent ramp of the dogwalk.

The handler must a) work for a solid contact performance, and then b) not allow the dog to run out too far after leaving the plank.

It might be in the handler's interest to use a hand signal and voice command for the pipe tunnel as they release from the dogwalk contact.

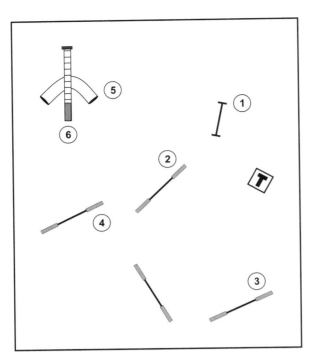

This contorted sequence opens with a depressed look at jump #2. The handler should not dismiss the off-course opportunity over the unlabeled jump.

The turn from #3 to #4 could go either right or left at the handler's option. Is one choice any better than the other?

Finally, (as though this sequence weren't exciting enough), the handler must put the dog up onto the dogwalk coming out of the tunnel. In this situation it would serve the handler to allow the dog to run out far enough to get a square approach to the walk, but not so far that the dog would be inclined to take an off-course jump.

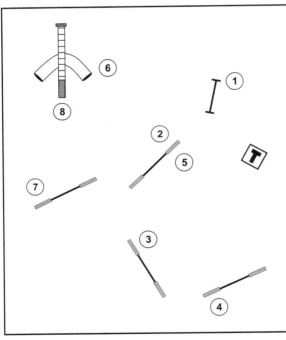

In this final sequence, a 270° turn is introduced in the transition from jump #3 to #4. The handler's choice of starting position will influence how the turn is negotiated. Take note of which starting side your students initially choose. Encourage them to experiment with starting the dog on either side.

The 270° turn will in many cases require the handler at least to run out past jump #3 to push the dog out and around for an approach to jump #4. Is anyone successful getting their dog out and around while remaining inside the jumps?

The exercise includes a minor discrimination between the pipe tunnel and dogwalk. If a dog takes the off-course dogwalk, take note of the handler's position. Chances are he was hanging back on the dog's left.

The final sequence pitches the dog out over jump #7 and then it's handler's choice in turning direction. Finish with the dogwalk framed by the off-course tunnel entries. A clean hand signal will be helpful.

# Set 3

Your set consists of four exercises. The first two exercises use the same equipment as do the last two exercises. However, major equipment movement is required between the second and third exercises. Brief your students immediately that they will be moving the equipment between exercises. You will lay the jump bars on the ground to indicate where to position jumps. Instruct your students to move the jump standards into place.

Balance your time with each group so that your students get approximately the same amount of work on each of the exercises.

## T Trouble

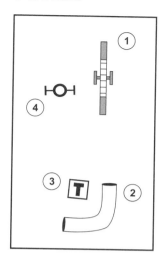

True teeter, tunnel, table and tire trouble, with a terrible twist. The table and pipe tunnel are set only about 2' apart so that it's a discrimination problem. Will the handler choose a blocking maneuver or choose body magnet to get the dog into the tunnel? How does the handler's choice of strategy influence which side the handler starts the dog on?

After your students are doing this exercise perfectly and feeling pretty cocky about it, reverse the numbering cones of #2 and #3 and do the exercise in this new sequence. Are they still feeling pretty cocky? How do the handlers deal with their dogs running past the table in transition from the pipe tunnel to the tire?

## More T Trouble

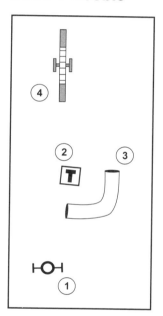

The biggest challenge in this set will be for the handler to get the dog past the inviting opening of the pipe tunnel and up on the table.

You should allow your students to handle the dog on either side and to lead out. Then, you should require them to do each.

If this is too easy, try this: Put *both* the #2 cone and the #3 cone on the pipe tunnel (same entry as #3 is now). The table will not be performed.

How will your students deal with this dilemma? Is turning left coming out of the tunnel on the first pass any safer than turning right? Have fun.

## Oopsi! Change of Direction

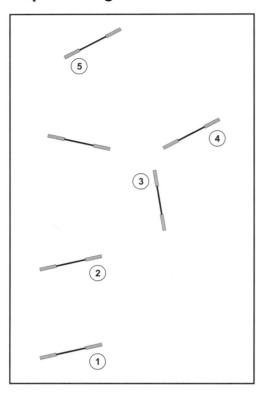

This jumping sequence features a 90° turn in the transition from jump #2 to jump #3. The mean judge has placed a dummy jump where #3 would be if there were *no* turn. Many of the dogs will take the dummy jump, even as their handlers take the turn.

This set will help your students work on this critical change of direction. Note that handling the dog on the obedience side and relying on *Come!* to change the dog's direction might not be the best choice for all dog and handler teams.

## Revisionist Oopsi!

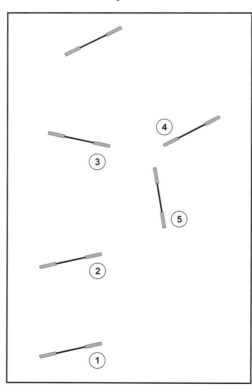

In this revisionist view of the Oopsi! set, the dog is presented with a long outrun and a last second change of direction.

Encourage your students to try *each* of these three handling techniques:

- **Start with the dog on the left**—The handler should rely on a strong *Come!* command to turn the dog into the pinwheel. Then the handler should suck back and somewhat to the right to influence the dog's turn.

- **Start with the dog on the right**—The handler should cross behind the dog after committing the dog out over jump #2.

- **Start with a lead-out**—The handler should get in front of the dog at jump #3, counter-rotating to push the dog out into the pinwheel.

WEEK 8

# Week 8: Student Notes

Many dogs are entered in their first agility trial with little or no event experience. An agility event is exciting and many new dogs get very distracted by all the excitement and commotion. So on the morning of the event, test your dog's ability to concentrate and his attentiveness to you by walking leisurely around the ring and the grounds with him on a loose lead. Randomly call the dog, *particularly* when something has interested him. If you find that your dog is suddenly oblivious to you, make yourself more enticing than the distraction (food, toy, silly behavior, leash pop, whatever works).

Repeat this many times until your dog is attentive on *you* (the handler) again. Last minute attention training such as this may help you to keep your dog's focus and avoid distraction when you attempt to run the course.

*Artist: Nancy Krouse-Culley*

## Gambler's Options

All of the exercises you've been doing to teach your dog to come, to get out, to go on, and to work away, culminate in your ability to actually control your dog at a distance, or at least to communicate to him your desires.

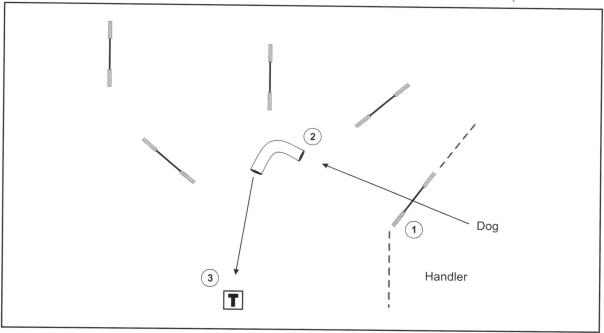

If you have already mastered the send to the tunnel, it should be fairly simple for you to be able to do this gamble. Notice the lines at the first jump. These restrict the handler's movement. You need to be able to send your dog over the jump and through the tunnel and onto the table, without crossing that line

It would be quite helpful for you to line your dog up as you approach the jump so that the tunnel is framed in the dog's vision between the standards of the jump. If you give him any other line to the opening jump whatever happens next could be more interesting than you really want it to be.

As the dog exits the tunnel, you could strike a path parallel to the dog's down the handler's line and give him the command to *Go! Table!*.

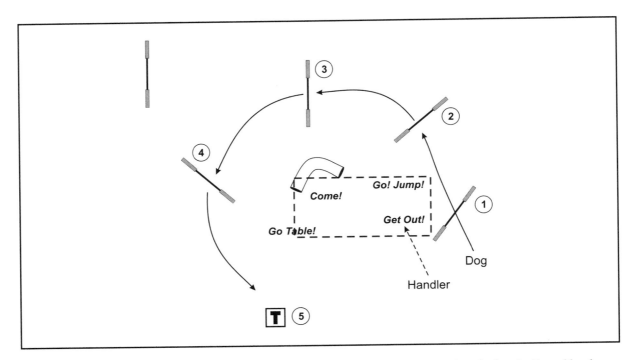

This is certainly a more complex and challenging gamble. The handler is restricted to the box indicated by the dashed outline. The handler can start with the dog behind the first jump; however, by the time the dog commits to jump #2 the handler must move into the box and stay there. Note that the box restricts the handler from moving on the outside of the tunnel.

The handler must use this narrowly defined space to move his body to communicate with the dog, and give a variety of commands in rapid succession as the dog negotiates the series of jumps to the table.

This performance uses the foundation of exercises that you have previously worked. And if you have taken your time and been patient with each of the exercises, then you have all of the commands in your repertoire to accomplish this gamble.

# Appendix

Identifying Motivation Problems

Enthusiasm Drills

Additional Guidelines for Program Design

Making Exercises More Complex

Additional Warm-Up Exercises

Crosses, Changes and Switches

Crossing Consternation

*Artist: Bud Houston*

# *Identifying Motivation Problems*

An agility instructor is called on to fix a myriad of problems related to performance. Why is a dog knocking poles? How do you get the dog to hit contacts? Why is the dog refusing the tire? In a way, these are the simplest problems to answer. We know how to do good foundation training, and obstacle performance problems usually relate to that foundation training. On the other hand there are many intangible performance problems, especially when it comes to motivation. Motivation problems are usually manifested in a dog's lack of speed, or refusing jumps and other obstacles. Following is an examination of possible problems.

**The dog is fearful of the equipment.** If a dog has been pushed along too quickly he might learn to fear the equipment. A sudden drop of the see-saw, loud noises, falling off the dogwalk... these are all events that could shape the dog's first impression of agility and make him fearful. It's difficult to instill in a dog that agility is fun when he's already made up his mind that it can be scary or painful. Although you can't control what an owner does with his dog at home, the instructor must always be sure that the training environment is safe and non-threatening for the dog.

**The dog is not fit.** A fat or out of shape dog is not going to much like this sport. Most exercises or even performances of individual obstacles can be quite demanding. Often the handler does not appreciate that his dog is fat or out of shape and will push the dog to overwork. The dog will quickly learn to dislike the sport. You really have to catch this problem before it ruins the dog on agility. You might even have a fitness test for dogs entering the program. Don't allow the fat dog. Tell the owner to go home and put the dog on a diet and do several months of reasonable road work. Tell them to come back again when they have their dog's in shape.

**The dog hurts.** Sometimes a dog has a physical malady that can make participating in agility not very fun. The dog may be dysplastic, or have a hurt back. You need to be able to recognize when a dog is hurting. It's possible for even a dysplastic dog to have a meaningful agility career if put on a conditioning program so that the dog's muscles and general fitness will protect him. But often the owner will not recognize the problem. You should counsel this owner to consult with a veterinarian and possibly put the dog on a conditioning program.

**The dog is afraid to make a mistake.** Some handlers are too quick to give their dogs an emotional or even a physical correction when the dog doesn't do an exercise as desired or expected. Yelling at a dog or hitting a dog will quickly convince the dog that doing agility isn't very fun. They will be so confused and disheartened when they are in class that it will be difficult for them to do anything right. An instructor needs to correct those handlers every time their voice gets gruff or any time they so much as pantomime hitting or threatening their dogs. Embarrass them in front of the group by pointing out their behavior. That should make them behave better in class, though you cannot control what they do at home. Point out to them that they are not helping their dogs to learn to do agility.

**The dog suffers from contrary conditioning.** Obedience trained dogs, especially, can have a hard time learning that it's okay to romp and play and work away from their handlers. They've been conditioned to stick like velcro to their handlers' legs, and know quite well the penalty for leaving this required position. The slower the obedience handler, then the slower the dog. This dog will move no faster than his own handler. This is really a difficult problem to break, but not impossible. You do the same foundation exercises. The only difference is that sometimes you have to do significantly more repetitions before the dog understands that he has permission to do something contrary to his obedience training. You should assign the "Enthusiasm Drills" on the next page as homework for this handler and dog team.

**The dog is uninspired and sees no point in the exercise.** Occasionally it's possible that the dog simply sees no point in the exercise and does not want to do it. This is a rarity, but it happens. You should counsel this handler to come to terms with the problem and realize that the dog will probably never excel in the sport. If the handler's intention is to win at the sport it is likely that they'll never do it with this dog. If the handler's objective is just to have a fun day in the park with the dog, then even slow and methodical play on an agility course is better than having the dog locked up in the backyard all day.

# *Enthusiasm Drills*

Let's first of all think about what enthusiasm means—It means how happy and motivated the dog is to go out and work with you. You can tell a lot about a dog's enthusiasm by the wag and movement of his tail, the bounce in his step, and the speed with which he commits to work.

If you come from an obedience background, there is a possibility that your dog has been taught all his life that it is against the rules to forge out ahead of you and strike his own eager path. Depending on your training methods, he may be fearful of making a mistake. This can lead him to move slowly and carefully and show a reluctance to take chances. So for the obedience dog, some "contrary conditioning" is called for.

Following are a series of enthusiasm drills. These are obstacle configurations that are calculated to make your dog have as much fun as possible. They minimize the possibility of failure, and are constructed so that your dog can build up speed—your ultimate objective.

Don't try to do all of these exercises on the same day. In fact, you really should take the long view in delivering this program. Spend a week with each exercise. Spend two weeks if you want. If the dog is familiar with the drill, he will consistently build confidence and speed.

Before beginning the exercises, you need to decide what kind of reward *really* excites your dog. It could be a toy. It could be food. It might be both. You decide. After you have made the decision, you will commit yourself to this essential principle:

> **You will praise your dog joyfully and give a reward for *every* repetition in the program. After you've been through the entire program, you can start thinking about cutting back on reward. If you are using a toy, you will immediately throw the toy for the dog as the dog clears the final hurdle of *every* repetition.**

Your objective is to get the dog anticipating the reward (and praise) so that he gets working in anticipation.

About jump heights—You aren't worrying about jump heights in these exercises. The purpose is *not* to work the dog at regulation height, but to get him working happily and fast. With this in mind, set the jumps low.

## Enthusiasm Exercise 1

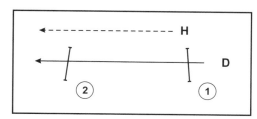

- Begin by running the sequence with your dog on the heel-side, giving the command for each jump. Praise the dog and give a reward after the second jump.

- After several repetitions with the dog on the heel-side, run the sequence with the dog on your right (the off-side). Praise the dog and give a reward after the second jump.

- Leave the dog in a sit-stay behind the first jump, lead out on the right, call your dog over the first jump, and then complete the sequence running with the dog as he performs the second jump.

- Leave the dog in a sit-stay behind the first jump, lead out on the left, call your dog over the first jump, and then complete the sequence running with the dog as he performs the second jump.

- Leave the dog in a sit-stay behind the first jump, lead out past both jumps, and call your dog over both jumps.

## Enthusiasm Exercise 2

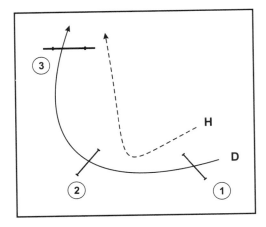

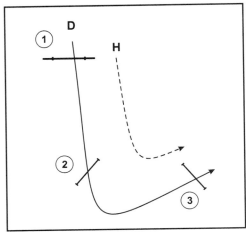

When doing this exercise you will *always* maintain the inside position, regardless of which side your dog will be working. The inside position allows you to take the shorter path, meaning that your dog will have to hurry to keep up with you.

- Do several repetitions with your dog working on the heel-side as shown in the first illustration. Praise the dog and give a reward after the third jump.

- Do several repetitions with your dog working on the off-side as shown in the second illustration. Praise the dog and give a reward after the third jump.

- Do several repetitions of the following: Begin with the dog on the heel-side and perform the three jumps. Immediately reverse direction after the last jump and do the three jumps with your dog on the off-side. Praise and reward.

- Do several repetitions of the following: Begin with the dog on the off-side and perform the three jumps. Immediately reverse direction after the last jump and do the three jumps with your dog on the heel-side. Praise and reward.

## Enthusiasm Exercise 3

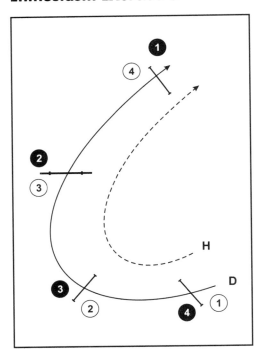

Again, when doing this exercise you will *always* maintain the inside position, regardless of which side your dog will be working.

- Do several repetitions with your dog working on the heel-side (white numbers in the illustration). Praise the dog and give a reward after the fourth jump.

- Do several repetitions with your dog working on the off-side (black numbers in the illustration). Praise the dog and give a reward after the third jump.

- Do several repetitions of the following: Begin with the dog on the heel-side and perform the four jumps. Immediately reverse direction after the last jump and do the four jumps with your dog on the off-side. Praise and reward.

- Do several repetitions of the following: Begin with the dog on the off-side and perform the four jumps. Immediately reverse direction after the last jump and do the four jumps with your dog on the heel-side. Praise and reward.

Advanced Agility Workbook

## Enthusisam Exercise 4

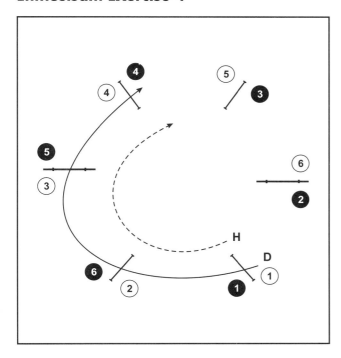

Again, when doing this exercise you will *always* maintain the inside position, regardless of which side your dog will be working.

- With the dog on the heel-side, put the dog over two jumps (white numbers) and then praise and reward.

- With the dog on the off-side, put the dog over two jumps (black numbers) and then praise and reward.

- With the dog on the heel-side, put the dog over four jumps and then praise and reward.

- With the dog on the off-side, put the dog over four jumps and then praise and reward.

- With the dog on the heel-side, put the dog over six jumps and then praise and reward.

- With the dog on the off-side, put the dog over six jumps and then praise and reward.

As you repeat this exercise, try to work closer and closer to the inside of the circle, putting more distance between you and your dog. This should be done very gradually! If your dog is slowing or showing any hesitation, work closer to the dog. Always be sure to keep your body rotated in the direction of the flow of the sequence.

## Enthusiasm Exercise 5

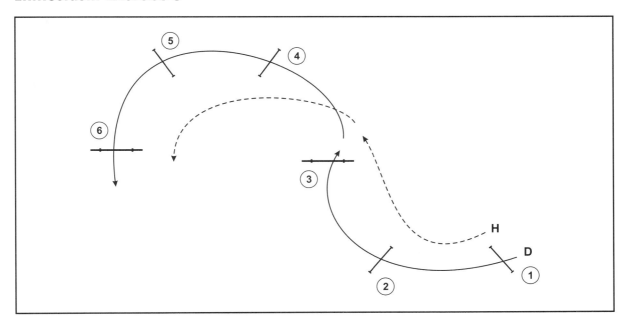

This exercise is designed to get your dog accustomed to the fact that you might change sides behind him. You will start with the dog on the heel-side and perform jumps #1–#3. As you commit your dog to jump #4, you will cross behind the dog so that he will be on your right for jumps #5 and #6. Praise and reward after the last jump. It will take lots of repetitions to get your dog comfortable with this manuever.

# Additional Guidelines for Program Design

A good agility training program is always evolving. You and your instructors should meet regularly to review training procedures and exercises, and to evaluate their effectiveness. The only way to discover what works and what doesn't work is to try out your ideas and carefully observe the results. When you design a new exercise does it accomplish the goal(s) you intended? Do your instructors understand the goal(s) of the exercise and are they comfortable running the set? How does the exercise work for the students? Is it over their heads? Is it too easy?

Throughout this workbook, we have suggested a number of guidelines for designing and structuring your advanced agility program. Here are a few other guidelines to keep in mind as you refine your program:

- Don't try to design a set of exercises to fix everyone's problems. It can't be done in an hour.

- Keep a training log of what the class has worked on lately. This will alert you as to obstacles and common obstacle configurations that you have neglected. For example, it's very easy to forget to set out the long jump. Then you and your students go to a trial where the judge seems determined to make up for all those other trials where he didn't use the long jump.

- After class, while it is still fresh, confer with the other instructors to determine if there is any pattern to the problems you are observing with the class. For example, if many dogs in the class are slow on the see-saw or knocking bars on the spread hurdle or can only make correct entry into the weaves if they are stopped or slowed down before the obstacle, you know that you have been neglecting this in your program. It is not a bad idea to keep notes on the individual students either. This can act as a rough metric so that you can measure whether or not your class is making progress in those long months between trial seasons.

- Keep copies of courses you have seen at trials. If you are having trouble thinking up a training pattern, these can be a good source of inspiration. Also, when designing exercise sets, it's easy to unconsciously lock yourself into using certain configurations; or not using certain configurations because you think of them as "unfair". Unfair or not, you and your students are going to see them at trial somewhere, so you may as well "Train, Don't Complain" as Jack Godsil used to say.

- Ask your students for feedback about what they liked and didn't like during the eight weeks. It's a good idea to develop an evaluation form that you give students on the last day of class.

# Making Exercises More Complex

Simplifying an exercise is easy—you straighten out the curves and make the sequence more straightforward. But, what do you do to make an exercise more complex, more challenging?

Let's face it, sometimes an advanced exercise turns out to be just another series of simple equipment performances. It becomes ho hum and not very challenging.

Following are eight recommendations for spicing up an exercise, to give it added meaning and challenge. Sometimes these tips will help make the exercise more fun, and almost always they will lead the students to discover something important in the working relationship with his dog.

**Silent Running**—Put up a sequence with multiple changes of side and discriminations. Require your students to run the exercise with no voice commands.

**The Surrogate Judge**—Dress up a "judge" in a big crinkly rain suit, a wide brimmed hat, floppy boots, and an umbrella. The judge will shadow the dog and handler around the course as they work. This is an invaluable exercise in getting the dog used to the omnipresent distraction of the judge in competition.

**Gambling**—Draw arbitrary containment lines on the sequence you are working. Advise your students that they can't pass that line. One variation is to give the students a platter which they may place anywhere in the sequence. But they must handle the entire sequence with one foot on the platter.

**Trading Places**—Make everyone in the class work a dog other than their own. Make the dog assignments in some tricky manner so that your students don't get to choose which dogs they will work.

**Tweaking**—You can always add complexity to a sequence simply by making the approaches to obstacles more difficult, shortening transitional distances, or adding obstacles to form options or discrimination problems. You can often reverse a sequence to explore new handling problems.

**Follow the Leader**—Just like the children's game of the same name, this exercise creates randomly generated complexity. The first player/handler does an obstacle; the next player/handler does that obstacle (in the same direction) and another obstacle; the third player and all subsequent players do the obstacles before them, and add one of their own. This game makes them pay attention and develop course memorization skills.

**Constraints**—The instructor always has the option to ask a student to try a different handling approach. For instance: start the sequence without a lead-out or try crossing in front of the dog rather than behind the dog. This is not to dictate a handling style, but to make the handler explore the possibilities and perhaps discover something useful.

**Listening**—Absurd as it sounds, you can occasionally find interesting complications from your students. They will often say something that opens the door to a unique challenge. And, you can always rely on the Socratic method: Ask your students "What would make this exercise more challenging?".

# Additional Warm-Up Exercises

The following exercises are designed to be used in place of the obedience-focused Control Exercises for Week 4 through Week 8 of this program, if you have enough equipment and space to set these up *in addition* to the weekly training sets.

## Warm-Up Exercise 1

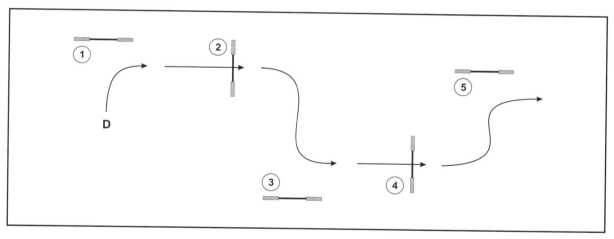

In the middle of the field, create the sequence of jumps in the illustration. These jumps will be used during the warm-up exercise.

- With all of the dogs on-lead, have your students free heel the dogs in a "follow-the-leader" fashion through the field of equipment. Allow the dogs to sniff and inspect the equipment. Take your time. Let the dogs get any desire to sniff and explore out of their systems.

  Now do the following exercise with all dogs in the class. Only one dog at a time will do the pattern, so organize your students into a line at the beginning. This exercise will be performed *off-lead*. The purpose of the exercise is to impress on the dog that sometimes the handler will want the dog to come (not perform an obstacle), and sometimes to go (and perform an obstacle).

- Have each handler heel his dog through this sequence, heeling the dog away from jumps #1, #3, and #5; and the last possible instant, performing jumps #2 and #4. Obviously handlers will have to get control of their dogs and resume heeling after the performance jumps.

- End of exercise. Praise the dogs and give them an appropriate reward.

## Warm-Up Exercise 2

In the middle of the field, create a wall of jumps with 5' to 10' between jumps. These jumps will be used during the warm-up exercise.

- With all of the dogs on-lead, have your students free heel the dogs in a "follow-the-leader" fashion through the field of equipment. Allow the dogs to sniff and inspect the equipment. Take your time. Let the dogs get any desire to sniff and explore out of their systems.

  Now, organize dogs and handlers into a long line facing the wall of jumps. There should be one dog for each jump in the line. The dogs will be *off-lead* for this exercise.

- Instruct your students to leave the dogs in a down-stay and walk away. Each handler should position himself halfway between his dog and the jump.

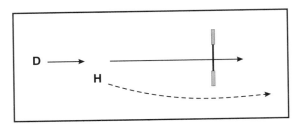

- One at a time, have your students recall their dogs. As the dog approaches, the handler spins toward the jump behind him and runs with the dog, instructing the dog to jump the hurdle. The handler should immediately get control of the dog, and form a line on the opposite side of the wall of jumps.

  After everyone has done the first part of this exercise, again have your students face the line of jumps.

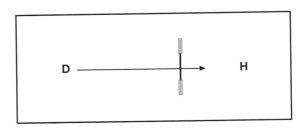

- Instruct your students to leave the dogs in a down-stay and walk to the *other* side of the line of jumps, putting a jump between himself and he dog.

- One at a time, have your students recall their dogs over the jumps.

- End of exercise. Praise the dogs and give them an appropriate reward.

## Warm-Up Exercise 3

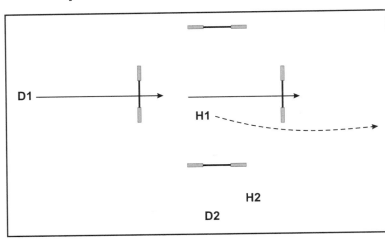

In the middle of the field, create a box of jumps with 20' across the box between the jumps. These jumps will be used during the warm-up exercise.

- With all of the dogs on-lead, have your students free heel the dogs in a "follow-the-leader" fashion through the field of equipment. Allow the dogs to sniff and inspect the equipment. Take your time. Let the dogs get any desire to sniff and explore out of their systems.

Advanced Agility Workbook

Now, organize dogs and handlers into two separate queues facing perpendicular sides of the box of jumps. Handlers from each line will alternately enter the box. The dogs will be *off-lead* for this exercise.

- Have a handler from the first queue leave his dog in a down-stay and then walk away from the dog into the box of jumps.

- Instruct the handler to recall his dog over the first jump. As the dog commits to the first jump, the handler spins toward the jump behind him and runs with the dog, instructing the dog to jump the second hurdle. The handler should immediately get control of the dog.

- Next have a handler from the second queue do essentially the same exercise

- Repeat this sequence until all dogs and handlers have had a turn.

- End of exercise. Praise the dogs and give them an appropriate reward.

**NOTE:** The purpose of having two lines is that the exercise can be done much more efficiently than if you only use one line. You keep both dogs and handlers moving, with constant action inside the box of jumps.

## Warm-Up Exercise 4

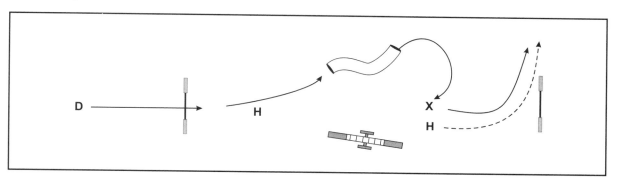

In the middle of the field, set up the sequence in the illustration. These obstacles will be used during the warm-up exercise.

- With all of the dogs on-lead, have your students free heel the dogs in a "follow-the-leader" fashion through the field of equipment. Allow the dogs to sniff and inspect the equipment. Take your time. Let the dogs get any desire to sniff and explore out of their systems.

  Now, organize dogs and handlers so that they are in line to begin of the exercise. The dogs will be *off-lead* for this exercise. One at a time, your students perform this sequence in the following manner:

- The handler puts his dog in a down-stay in front of the opening jump.

- The handler leads out around the jump and then calls his dog over the jump.

- The handler immediately spins and sends his dog to the second obstacle (either the tunnel or the see-saw).

- After the second obstacle, the handler calls the dog back to position "X", gains control of the dog, and puts the dog into heel position.

- The handler heels his dog directly towards the final jump and at the last minute heels/turns the dog away from the jump.

- End of exercise. Praise the dog and give him an appropriate reward.

**Warm-Up Exercise 5**

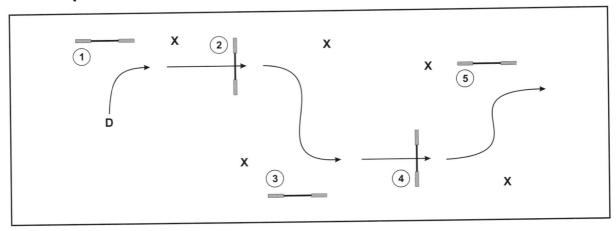

In the middle of the field, create the sequence of jumps in the illustration. These jumps will be used during the warm-up exercise. In addition, at every point in the sequence marked by "X", place a plate with food treats. These will be a test of the dog's ability to work with a major distraction nearby.

- With all of the dogs on-lead, have your students free heel the dogs in a "follow-the-leader" fashion through the field of equipment. Allow the dogs to sniff and inspect the equipment. Take your time. Let the dogs get any desire to sniff and explore out of their systems.

  Do the following exercise with all dogs in the class. Only one dog at a time will do the pattern, so organize your students into a line at the beginning. The dogs will be *off-lead* for this exercise. The purpose of the exercise is to impress on the dog that sometimes the handler will want the dog to *come* (not perform an obstacle), and sometimes to *go* (and perform an obstacle).

- Have each handler heel his dog through this sequence, heeling the dog away from jumps #1, #3, and #5; and the last possible instant, performing jumps #2 and #4. Obviously handlers will have to get control of their dogs and resume heeling after the performance jumps.

- End of exercise. Praise the dogs and give them an appropriate reward (unless they have already adequately rewarded themselves).

**NOTE:** Make sure the bait plates, marked by the positions "X", contain food treats for each dog. This is intended to be a fun exercise. Don't allow harsh corrections for dogs that do the natural thing and prefer the bait plates to their handler's company.

# Crosses, Changes and Switches

A handler may choose strategic changes of sides to manage the dog's flow through a sequence of obstacles. It's possible that in the Novice or Starters ranks, a dog and handler team can earn an agility title by running the dog exclusively on the obedience side. But in Open/Advanced and Excellent/Masters classes, the complexity of the courses and the demands of the standard course time require the handler to add smart working habits to his handling repertoire.

A change of sides often allows the handler to take a path shorter than that the dog must take. A change of sides can communicate a change of direction to the dog or effectively communicate the correct path through options and traps.

The following examples and definitions are intended to illustrate the many possibilities for crosses, changes, and switches. Use this as a reference for identifying and setting up training challenges.

## Static Cross

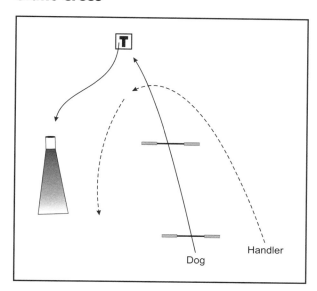

A **static cross** is when the handler switches sides to his dog while the dog is in a stationery or static position, such as on the table. In this illustration, you can see that the dog begins the series of jumps on the handler's left side. But while the dog is on the table, the handler turns between the table and the jump so that the dog will be on his right side when the dog gets off the table.

The handler could use the dog's static position to get a lead-out advantage to direct the dog down field. However, this is possible only if the dog will remain in the down or sit required by the judge. Some handlers will get the dog pointing in the direction of the continuing flow before commanding the dog to *Down!* (or *Sit!*) on the table, so that the dog doesn't break position as he looks over his shoulder while the handler takes a lead-out.

## Dynamic Cross

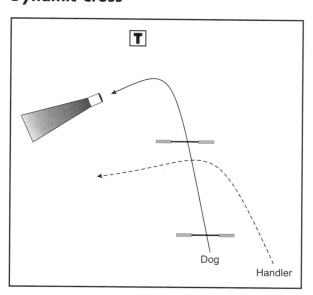

A **dynamic cross** occurs when the handler switches sides to the dog while the dog is in motion *and* while the dog can see the handler.

In this example, the handler crosses the dog's path to direct the dog onto a new course, and hopefully away from an off-course possibility. Some dogs are very sensitive to the handler's movement when the handler crosses behind, and will quickly change directions to take up the same path as the handler.

See "Crossing Behind".

## Blind Cross

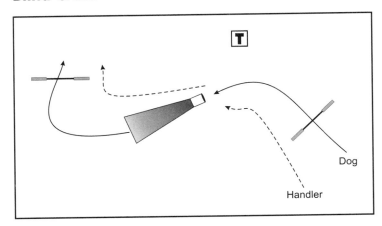

A **blind cross** occurs when the handler switches sides to his dog while the dog is in a tunnel and therefore cannot see the handler. The dog is "blind" to the handler's movement.

You can see in the illustration that the handler starts with the dog on his right, pauses briefly to get his dog into the tunnel, and then quickly steps up around the tunnel to change direction and switch sides.

When working the collapsed tunnel in this fashion, the handler should speak to the dog while he's inside the tunnel to announce the change of sides. This will help the dog turn efficiently out of the tunnel.

The purpose of a blind cross is for the handler to cross in front of the  tunnel rather than running around it, thus giving the handler a shorter path to run.

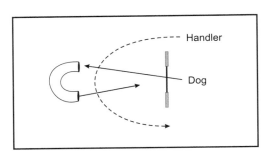

In this illustration, the handler actually crosses his dog's path *twice*, once behind the dog and once in front. This maneuver allows the handler to take the shorter path.

If one of your students chooses to run *around* the pipe tunnel, the only effective corrective action would be to make liberal fun of them, or to beat them with a rattan cane.

## Axford Axel

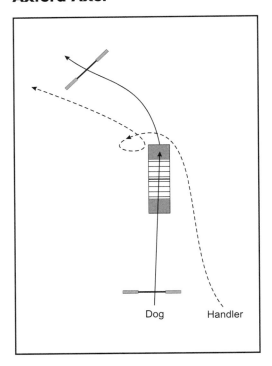

The **Axford Axel** is a counter-rotation and side switch at the descent side of a contact obstacle, or at the end of the weave poles. Many dogs perform the A-frame very quickly. Therefore, if the handler executes an Axford Axel, the timing must be very good so that dog and handler don't collide on the descent. Certainly if this maneuver were performed on the see-saw (or, arguably, the dogwalk) the handler will have more time to make the turn.

As with any counter-rotation, the handler turns toward the dog so that his back is never to his dog.

This maneuver can also be effective to make a dog with a down-side contact problem get a paw in the yellow. As the handler pivots in front of his dog, they come eyeball to eyeball. This moment will make many dogs pause, and perform the contact without fault.

## Crossing Behind

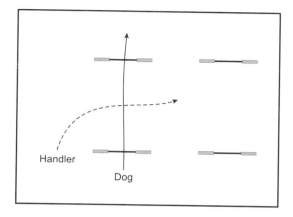

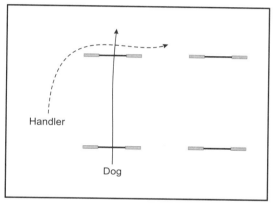

In crossing *behind* the dog, the handler commits his dog to the next obstacle in sequence and then switches sides.

Several problems can result from crossing behind a dog:

- A dog could pull off the obstacle, earning a refusal, after sensing the change in the handler's direction.

- The dog might shorten stride, slowing down, on the approach to the obstacle. A knocked bar is likely.

- The dog might *not* sense the handler's change of sides and will turn the wrong direction, or float out too far before being called back. This is an inefficient turn that wastes valuable seconds.

Note that a cross behind does not refer in any way to the obstacle. In this illustration the handler chooses to cross behind his dog *after* the jump. This choice is often necessary in the case of a dog that will not work ahead of his handler. If the handler stops in front of the dog, waiting to cross behind before the jump, the dog will also stop. This handler needs to learn to run *past* the jump before crossing.

This maneuver can also be performed off a contact obstacle. After the dog hits the contact, the handler commits forward a bit. When the dog moves forward, the handler steps in behind the dog and off in a new direction.

## Crossing In Front

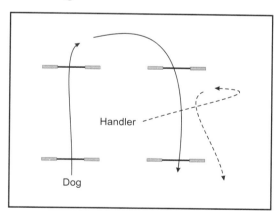

A handler crosses in front by switching sides *in front* of the dog. In this illustration, the handler sends his dog out to perform a 180° turn. The handler counter-rotates so that the dog focuses on the jump and is redirected into the correct course flow.

As with all counter-rotations, the handler never turns his back on the dog.

A dog typically works with greater speed if the handler can find a way to cross in front. In addition, the handler will be better positioned to direct the dog into the continuing flow of the course.

## Counter-Rotation

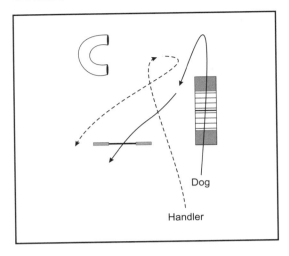

Dog

Handler

A **counter-rotation** is a pivot or pirouette performed by the handler to reverse the direction of flow. The handler should *never* turn his back on his dog (otherwise it isn't a counter-rotation).

The counter-rotation has been used in several different illustrations in this text. This illustration shows how the maneuver can remove the possibility of an off-course if used properly.

The handler might have chosen to turn on axis and call the dog around him counter-clockwise using *Come!* to keep the dog turning. That method, however, would have presented the pipe tunnel *twice* as an off-course possibility. The counter-rotation, however, manages the dog's path so that the pipe tunnel is never really presented to the dog.

# *Crossing Consternation*

*by Monica Percival*

The following are the 10 most popular reasons that people give me to explain why they can't cross in front of their dogs:

1.  Your dog wouldn't like it and might get mad at you.

2.  You couldn't possibly get comfortable doing it.

3.  You'll get in your dog's way and he'll bump into you (possibly earning a fault).

4.  Your dog will get in your way and you'll trip over him and fall down (exposing yourself to the potential for serious injury or embarassment).

5.  A wise agility veteran told you never to do it.

6.  No one else in your training group does it.

7.  You have an open dog and only mini-dog handlers do that sort of thing (*real* open handlers always cross behind their dogs).

8.  You'll obstruct your dog's vision and he won't be able to see where he's going.

9.  You are too slow.

10. Your dog is too fast.

I'm used to dealing with a little skepticism from advanced students when I introduce new training ideas; however, I've never had students react so strongly to a concept as they do when I start talking about crossing in front of a dog. Students go into great detail about why it can't and shouldn't be done—of course, most of them have never tried it. So I started thinking...is it possible that people don't understand the basic concept? Crossing in front of your dog does *not* mean racing the dog from point A to point B and then trying to cut in front of him! So what does it mean?

In any sequence or course, there's a path that you want the dog to take. Whenever you change handling sides, you cross this path. Crossing in front of the dog means that you change sides by crossing this path at a point where the dog has not yet travelled. Crossing behind the dog means that you change sides by crossing this path at a point that the dog has already passed.

Advanced Agility Workbook

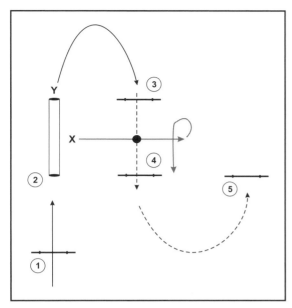

This illustration shows an example of crossing in front. The dog's path is shown with the black line. The solid black line represents the path that the dog has already travelled and the dashed black line represents the dog's intended path that he hasn't yet travelled. The handler's path is shown with the grey dashed line.

Starting at "X", the handler calls the dog over jump #1 and into the tunnel (dog is on handler's left). While the dog is in the tunnel moving towards point "Y", the handler moves as shown by the dashed line and crosses the dog's path at the point indicated by the black circle—the dog hasn't yet travelled this part of the path so the handler has just crossed in front of his dog.

Positioning himself on the far side of jumps #3 and #4, the handler rotates towards the dog until he is facing jump #4; calls the dog over jump #3 (dog is now on handler's right); and then sends the dog over jump #4.

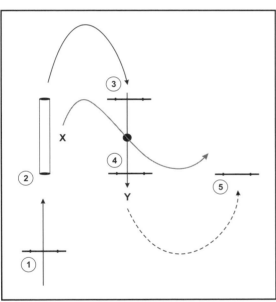

This illustration shows an example of crossing behind. The handler starts at point "X"; calls the dog over jump #1 and into the tunnel (dog is on handler's left); pushes the dog out for an approach to jump #3; rotates away from the dog towards jump #4; calls the dog over jump #3; and then sends the dog over jump #4 off his left side.

As the dog approaches point "Y", the handler moves as shown by the grey dashed line and crosses the dog's path at the point indicated by the black circle—the dog has already travelled this part of the path so the handler has just crossed behind the dog. The handler rotates away from the dog again (dog is now on the handler's right) and calls the dog over jump #5.

Changing sides by crossing in front of your dog is *not* a replacement for crossing behind. On an actual course it's impossible—and certainly not desirable—to cross in front of your dog at every point that offers an opportunity to cross behind. However, the possibility of crossing in front of your dog, is one that most people ignore when they walk a course; and it's a handling technique that can produce very good results in many situations. But like any other handling technique, you need to practice it and figure out when it's a good strategy and when it's not.

What can be some of the advantages to crossing in front?

- It can allow you to lead your dog through a difficult portion of a course rather than trying to guide him from behind.

- It can allow your dog to make smoother transitions between obstacles and it can prevent some dogs from spinning as they change direction.

- It can make parts of a course flow better, which will help keep slower dogs moving.

APPENDIX

- It can help you slow down a very fast dog and control his approach to an obstacle.

- It gives you an alternative for a dog that refuses to get comfortable with you crossing behind or for a dog that doesn't have the forward propulsion necessary for you to send him ahead and cross behind.

Stuart Mah of Stars and Stripes Agility in Chino, California designed an exercise called "Oscillations". This exercise is shown in the illustration below. During the past month, I've introduced the exercise to a number of students and their dogs and have noted the results. I've also experimented with the dogs in my own house. If you haven't tried this exercise with your students, I highly recommend it. Set it up and let them run it. At first, don't give them any indication of how you want them to run it.

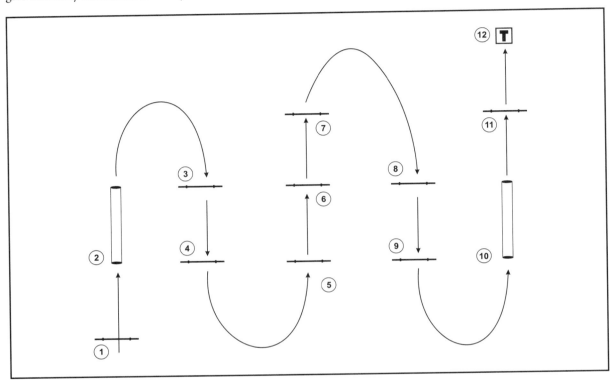

All of my students initially attempted to cross behind their dogs. I let them run the exercise several times this way, but the results were poor in general. So I suggested that there was an alternative handling strategy. Without telling them what I was doing, I ran the same sequence with my dog, crossing in front rather than behind. All of the students were excited and wanted to try it this way. I had them walk the sequence without their dogs and plan their crosses. When they tried the alternative—crossing in front—the results were much more positive. This held true regardless of a dog's experience, jump height, or speed. They were all shocked when I explained that they had just successfully crossed in front of their dogs!

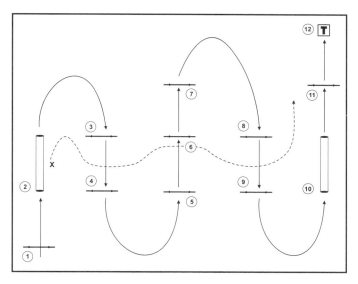

This illustration shows the handling path that my students initially chose. Starting at "X", the handler calls the dog over jump #1 and into the tunnel. The handler pushes the dog out for an approach to jump #3; rotates *away* from the dog towards jump #4; and calls the dog over jump #3. As the handler sends the dog over jump #4, he crosses behind the dog; calls the dog over jump #5; sends the dog over jumps #6 and #7 (the handler may have to go closer to jump #7 than shown); and then crosses behind the dog. The handler rotates *away* from the dog towards jump #9; calls the dog over jump #8; sends the dog over jump #9; crosses behind the dog once again; and then sends the dog through the closing sequence.

When crossing behind their dogs, my students experienced problems ranging from dogs spinning as they changed direction to dogs going off-course. When I duplicated their handling path with my Border Collie, "Lazer," the results were not any better—in fact, his extreme speed and tendency to jump long made the problems even worse.

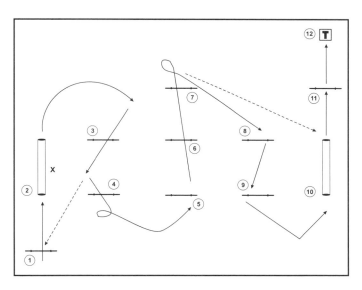

The illustration on the left shows how crossing behind Lazer in this exercise effected his path. In the opening sequence, Lazer had so much speed through the tunnel that he swung very wide in his approach to jump #3 (despite my tight rotation towards jump #4). This set him up for jump #3 at an acute angle and put jump #1 in his line of sight. (The first time through he actually did back-jump #1.) Because the transition from #3 to #4 was so angular, it was hard for me to cross without having Lazer spin after jump #4.

Jumps #5 through #7 went well each time since Lazer is easy to send out ahead in a straight line. However, if I didn't come to a stand still after crossing behind him at jump #6, any subsequent movement on my part would push Lazer out too far or off-course. (The first time through he took the wrong end of the tunnel at #10 after jumping #7.) Again, we experienced a spinning problem after jump #7. The closing sequence was uneventful. Despite repeating the exercise many times, the results did not get significantly better.

Some general observations about crossing behind Lazer in this sequence were that:

- My rotations had to be even tighter than usual in order to turn the dog fast enough and keep him from swinging too wide.

- There was no room for error in the timing of my crosses. If I was still moving after a cross, I would inevitably push the dog out too far or to the wrong obstacle. If I didn't move fast enough, I would cause the dog to spin after a jump (sometimes knocking a bar) because he wouldn't pick up my new position in time to make a smooth turn.

- Even when we were getting the sequence right each time, it didn't feel good. I was uncomfortable and felt like I was struggling to keep control of the dog. The dog's path seemed too "choppy" and angular.

- The dog was covering far more ground than I would have liked.

Among my students and my other dogs, these observations held true even for slower or less experienced dogs. Where fast dogs went wide, slower dogs also went wide—in fact, many slowed down even more as they made these wide arcs. The slow dogs were also just as likely to spin when they changed direction as the fast dogs.

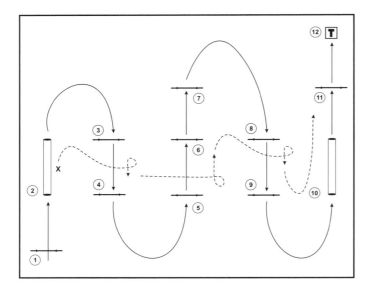

This illustration shows the path (the dashed line) that I had my students try next. Starting at "X" and facing jump #3, the handler calls the dog over jump #1 and into the tunnel. While the dog is in the tunnel, the handler moves across to the far side of jumps #3 and #4; turns his body (towards the dog) until it's square to jump #4; calls the dog over jump #3; and then sends the dog over jump #4.

As soon as the dog commits to jump #4, the handler must "slide" down the handling line to the far side of jumps #5 through #7; turn towards the dog until he faces jump #6; call the dog over jump #5; and then send the dog over jumps #6 and #7 (some handlers may need to move toward jump #7 to push the dog out far enough).

When the dog commits to jump #7, the handler slides over to the far side of jumps #8 and #9; turns to face jump #9; calls the dog over jump #8; sends him over jump #9; and then turns the dog into the closing sequence. In this scenario, the handler is always turning towards the dog or counter-rotating.

When I used this technique with Lazer, his path flowed smoothly from obstacle to obstacle with good efficient turns and straight lines between the jumps. As I repeated the exercise with Lazer, I made several observations:

- Despite the fact that I'm slow and he's fast, I was always able to make the cross. In general, there was a lot more room for error in my timing. I could still be in motion after the cross because the dog was still being drawn in the right direction—towards me!

- He changed direction smoothly and did not spin. The dog's turns were tighter and he covered much less ground than when I had been crossing behind.

All in all, it felt good to run the exercise this way. My students all had similar experiences. While they were initially uncomfortable since they had never practiced this technique, in the end, they all said that "it felt better."

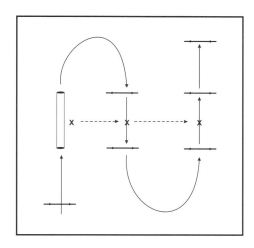

With Lazer and other fast dogs, I found several other ways to use crossing in front to the handler's advantage. Instead of crossing to the far side of each line of jumps, I crossed to the center as shown by the "X"s in the illustration on the left. For example, in the opening sequence, I moved in between jumps #3 and #4; faced the dog as he approached jump #3; and called him over the jump.

By cutting down the amount of space where Lazer had to land after jump #3 (position "X" cuts the landing space in half), he shortened his stride and eased his approach to the jump. By facing the dog, I could give him a strong *easy* command to also help quiet his approach. As he committed to jump #3, I stepped aside, rotated, and squared my body to jump #4. The longer I held my position at "X", the more I was able to control the dog's approach to the jump.

By easing Lazer's approach to jump #3 and shortening his landing, I also improved his approach to jump #4 so he was able to make a tight turn into jump #5. I repeated these techniques throughout the sequence. The dog had to cover much less ground and all the jump poles were in place as the dog had jumped much more carefully.

So what's the moral of this long story? Don't dismiss any handling technique until you've spent some time experimenting with how it works with *your* dog in different situations. Keep your eyes and your mind open when you walk a course—crossing behind will often work, but you may start noticing sequences where you could cross in front of the dog and end up ahead of the game.

*Artist: Jaci Cotton*